New
TEXAS HISTORY
MOVIES

Drawings and Text by

JACK JACKSON

Introduction by

JOHN WHEAT

Texas State Historical Association

Austin

Copyright ©2007 by the Texas State Historical Association

Library of Congress Cataloging-in-Publication Data

Jackson, Jack, 1941–2006
  New Texas History Movies / drawings and text by Jack Jackson; introduction by John Wheat.
  p. cm.
Includes bibliographical references.
ISBN 978-0-87611-223-6 (alk. paper)
  1. Texas—History—Juvenile literature. 2. Texas—History—Pictorial works—Juvenile literature. 3.
Texas—History—Caricatures and cartoons—Juvenile literature. I. Texas State Historical
Association. II. Title.

F386.3.J32 2007
976.4—dc22   2006038402

          5   4   3   2   1   07   08   09   10   11

Published by the Texas State Historical Association
Designed by David Timmons.

INTRODUCTION

JACK JACKSON ("Jaxon") left us a rich legacy of both art and historical writing. The academic community lauded his award-winning scholarly works, but a wider public marveled at his series of cartoon histories of Texas. There, Jackson married his intricate pen-and-ink graphics with painstaking historical research to create compelling historical narratives about Comanches, Tejanos, and even un-Reconstructed Anglo racists.

Jackson had nurtured the idea of the cartoon history since he first read the classic *Texas History Movies* as a schoolboy in South Texas. Though he disliked their cultural biases and racial stereotyping, he understood both the popular appeal and the narrative power of that medium. One critical analysis of comic books as history places Jackson among those artists who have developed the comic book from escapist entertainment to a new medium of visual and literary expression embracing serious historical themes, such as the clash of cultures in the American Southwest. "Jackson's achievement is to write narratives in the sequential art medium which introduce to the culture at large previously marginalized figures of American history."[1]

Jack Jackson died in June 2006. In his last work he revisited the old *Texas History Movies* and, despite the muscular degeneration of his hands, painstakingly recreated the cartoon history of Texas the way he always envisioned it: balanced and fair, warts and all, artfully drawn, and eminently readable. *New Texas History Movies* is a fitting testament to a life filled with art and history, and Jackson's final gift to us all.

John Wheat
Center for American History
University of Texas at Austin

[1] Joseph Witek, *Comic Books as History: The Narrative Art of Jack Jackson, Art Spiegelman, and Harvey Pekar* (Jackson, MS: University Press of Mississippi, 1989), 61.

IN FOURTEEN HUNDRED AND NINETY-TWO, COLUMBUS SAILED THE OCEAN BLUE.

If the earth is round, I can reach the east by heading west.

THIS WAS A REVOLUTIONARY IDEA, NOT ACCEPTED AT THE TIME.

HE MADE LANDFALL IN THE BAHAMAS, THINKING HE HAD REACHED THE RICH SPICE ISLANDS OF ASIA.

...in the name of Isabella of Castile and Ferdinand of Aragon.

CUBA AND HAITI WERE ALSO DISCOVERED ON THIS VOYAGE.

I want these people to be friendly to us, so don't cheat them while trading.

IN 1493 COLUMBUS RETURNED TO SPAIN WITH SOME EXOTIC ITEMS BUT LITTLE GOLD.

Haiti has many gold mines. It is near another island where there is gold without limit.

Then why have you brought back only a handful to your royal sovereigns?

Majesty, it would have taken me 50 years to explore all the islands I discovered.

...but I've brought back these Indians to learn our language, to serve as interpreters on my return voyage.

IN 1500 COLUMBUS WAS ARRESTED BY A NEW GOVERNOR AND SENT BACK TO SPAIN TO FACE CHARGES SUCH AS ENSLAVING THE INDIANS.

HE LOST FAVOR AT COURT BUT WAS PERMITTED TO MAKE ONE LAST VOYAGE IN 1502, MOSTLY TO BE RID OF HIS CONSTANT DEMANDS.

Tell him he must not bring back any slaves!

THE AGING ADMIRAL HOPED TO REGAIN HIS REPUTATION BY MAKING A MAJOR DISCOVERY BUT FAILED IN THE ATTEMPT. HE DIED 4 YEARS LATER.

There must be a strait that leads to the Orient.

OTHER SPANIARDS FOLLOWED COLUMBUS'S LEAD. IN 1519 HERNAN CORTES LANDED AN ARMY ON THE MAINLAND OF MEXICO NEAR MODERN VERACRUZ.

Sink the ships so there will be no turning back.

CORTES MADE ALLIES WITH THE HELP OF LA MALINCHE, A NATIVE WOMAN.

Many tribes hate the Aztecs.

THE AZTECS HAD ALL THE GOLD THAT COLUMBUS HAD HOPED TO FIND BUT MISSED. WITH HIS INDIAN ALLIES, CORTES CONQUERED MEXICO CITY TWO YEARS LATER.

Look at that!

Grander than the cities back home.

BY 1525 ALL EUROPE WAS TALKING ABOUT THE TREASURES OF THE NEW WORLD.

They eat off plates of solid gold!

Well, what are we waiting for?

THE NARVAEZ EXPEDITION OF 1528 REACHED FLORIDA BUT MET WITH DISASTER. SURVIVORS TRIED TO ESCAPE BY WATER.

We'll skirt the coastline to Mexico.

TWO OF THEIR BARGES WERE WRECKED NEAR GALVESTON ISLAND AND MOST OF THE SPANIARDS DIED.

Our prospects are not good.

KARANKAWA INDIANS TRIED TO HELP THE STARVING SURVIVORS, ONE OF WHOM WAS CABEZA DE VACA.

Eat! Sardine tasty.

CABEZA DE VACA LIVED AND TRADED WITH THE TEXAS INDIANS FOR OVER SIX YEARS.

Now here's a great deal for you.

HE GAINED A REPUTATION AMONG THEM AS A HEALER OF THE SICK AND INJURED.

FINALLY, IN 1536, CABEZA DE VACA AND SEVERAL COMPANIONS REACHED OTHER SPANIARDS NEAR THE WEST COAST.

What? Are you men like us?

CABEZA DE VACA WAS THE FIRST EUROPEAN TO WRITE ABOUT HIS EXPERIENCES IN TEXAS.

Yeah but don't ask me to go back there.

ALTHOUGH GOLD WAS ALWAYS THE OBJECT SOUGHT, RICH SILVER STRIKES CAUSED THE SPANIARDS TO PLANT SETTLEMENTS NORTH OF MEXICO CITY.

There's plenty more where this came from.

RUMORS OF GREATER RICHES PUSHED THEM EVER NORTHWARD TOWARD THE SEVEN CITIES OF CIBOLA.

Amazing, isn't it?

Yes, and it's the smallest of the Seven Cities.

Tell us what you saw Fray Marcos.

At sunset the city gleamed like gold.

FRANCISCO VAZQUEZ DE CORONADO SET OUT IN 1540 TO FIND THIS WEALTH. ONE OF HIS SCOUTING PARTIES SAW THE GRAND CANYON.

Quite a drop from here.

NEAR ALBUQUERQUE, NEW MEXICO, CORONADO MET AN INDIAN WHO CLAIMED TO KNOW ABOUT THE RICHES OF HIS BIRTHPLACE, QUIVIRA.

They store their corn in giant bowls made out of gold.

Really?

CORONADO FOLLOWED THE TURK EASTWARD ACROSS THE TEXAS PANHANDLE TOWARD KANSAS.

Just a little further.

BUT THE EXPEDITION FOUND NO GOLD, JUST ENDLESS PLAINS AND HOSTILE INDIANS.

You tricked me. Admit it!

AT THE SAME TIME THAT CORONADO WAS TRAVELING EAST, PART OF HERNANDO DE SOTO'S EXPEDITION WAS WORKING ITS WAY WEST FROM THE MISSISSIPPI RIVER.

Mexico must be somewhere in this direction.

THIS CAMPAIGN, LED BY LUIS DE MOSCOSO, REACHED THE CADDOAN TRIBES OF EAST TEXAS BEFORE TURNING BACK.

He says the Indians south of here don't grow corn and are very warlike.

APART FROM THESE BRIEF VISITS, THE INDIANS OF TEXAS WERE LEFT PRETTY MUCH TO THEMSELVES FOR THE NEXT 150 YEARS. THE APACHES CONTINUED TO HUNT BUFFALO ON FOOT.

THE KARANKAWAS WERE MASTERS OF THEIR COASTAL HABITAT. THEY PLUNDERED WRECKED VESSELS WHEN THE OPPORTUNITY PRESENTED ITSELF.

All we need now is the horse.

Alligator grease keeps off the mosquitoes.

THE SOUTH TEXAS TRIBES, COMPOSED OF VARIOUS GROUPS AND GENERALLY CALLED COAHUILTECANS, LIVED MUCH AS THEY HAD IN CABEZA DE VACA'S TIME.

THE WANDERING PLAINS TRIBES CARRIED ON A BRISK TRADE WITH THE SETTLED AGRICULTURAL TRIBES OF EAST TEXAS.

Well, this is the last of the mesquite bean casserole.

I know! Let's go visit Kwachi and see if the pecans are ripe yet.

Seven buffalo robes for one lousy jug? C'mon!

Okay, I'll throw in a pumpkin, how's that?

THE JUMANOS ALONG THE MIDDLE RIO GRANDE BUILT ADOBE HOUSES AND RAISED CORN, BEANS, AND SQUASH.

WALLS OF CAVES WERE OFTEN PAINTED WITH RELIGIOUS ART, SEEKING SUCCESSFUL HUNTS FROM THE SPIRIT WORLD.

Eat your vegetables, my momma always said.

You got his horns way too small!!

Yeah, he was a 12-pointer at least!

Critics, bah!

MEANWHILE, TREASURE SHIPS REGULARLY SAILED TO SPAIN FROM MEXICO.

THIS UPSET THE FRENCH SUN KING, LOUIS XIV, WHO DECIDED TO ESTABLISH A COLONY ON THE LOWER MISSISSIPPI RIVER IN 1684.

THE BRAINS BEHIND THE SCHEME WAS SIEUR DE LA SALLE, WHO HAD FLOATED ALL THE WAY DOWNRIVER FROM CANADA TWO YEARS EARLIER.

Yo ho ho and a bottle of rum.

It's not fair for Spain to hog all the gold and silver in America!

Not fair at all, Your Majesty!

See? From the river's mouth it's only a short trip to the rich Spanish mines.

My, that is close.

4

LA SALLE THOUGHT THAT THE MISSISSIPPI ENTERED THE GULF RIGHT NEXT TO THE RIO GRANDE.

SO HE WENT ASHORE AT MATAGORDA BAY, FIGURING IT WAS THE MISSISSIPPI DELTA, AND HIS SHIPS SAILED BACK TO FRANCE.

THUS BEGAN THE FIRST SETTLEMENT OF EUROPEANS IN TEXAS.

IT DIDN'T TAKE LA SALLE LONG TO REALIZE THAT HE WAS LOST.

WHILE LA SALLE LOOKED FOR THE MIGHTY MISSISSIPPI, SO HE COULD REACH CANADA AND GET HELP, HIS COLONISTS SUFFERED FROM SICKNESS AND STARVATION.

ON ONE OF THESE EXPLORATIONS, LA SALLE WAS KILLED NEAR THE BRAZOS RIVER BY SOME OF HIS MEN.

THE INDIANS FINISHED OFF WHAT WAS LEFT OF HIS PITIFUL COLONY, BUT A FEW PEOPLE MANAGED TO SURVIVE.

WORD OF LA SALLE'S DARING VENTURE SOON REACHED OFFICIALS IN NEW SPAIN, AS MEXICO WAS CALLED IN THOSE DAYS.

INDIAN GUIDES WERE USED ON THE FIRST SPANISH ATTEMPTS TO LOCATE THE FRENCH IN THE UNCHARTED WILDERNESS.

ON HIS FOURTH EXPEDITION IN 1689, GEN. ALONSO DE LEON FINALLY FOUND THE FRENCH FORT.

Not much to see after all our tramping around in th' brush.

TWO FRENCH YOUTHS WERE RECOVERED FROM THE INDIANS.

We've heard about others.

DE LEON CAME BACK A YEAR LATER, TO BURN WHAT WAS LEFT OF THE RUINS. THEN HE WENT FURTHER NORTH, TO THE NECHES RIVER, AND ESTABLISHED A MISSION FOR THE CADDO INDIANS.

Techas! Techas!!

I think the word means 'friends,' Your Grace.

How nice.

MORE FRENCH CAPTIVES WERE RESCUED FROM THE INDIANS ON THIS 1690 EXPEDITION.

Robert, how you've grown!

BUT THIS MISSION, AND OTHERS SOON FOUNDED IN EAST TEXAS, DID NOT PROSPER.

You must change your pagan ways.

THE CADDOAN GROUPS REFUSED TO ABANDON THEIR FIELDS AND RESETTLE NEAR THE MISSIONS.

And we're happy with our own religion, thank you.

SICKNESS AMONG THE INDIANS AND OTHER DIFFICULTIES SOON CAUSED THE MISSIONARIES TO WITHDRAW.

Bury the bells until we can make another try.

WHEN THE EAST TEXAS MISSIONS WERE CLOSED IN 1693, THE KING'S HIGHWAY GREW UP WITH WEEDS AND STAYED THAT WAY FOR TWENTY YEARS.

Hard to tell where it came thru here.

I sure miss that candy the priests used to give us.

THEN, IN 1714, A YOUNG FRENCHMAN NAMED SAINT-DENIS CAME DOWN THE TRAIL FROM LOUISIANA TO TRADE WITH THE SPANIARDS.

♫ I see miles an' miles of Texas ♫

WHILE AT SAN JUAN BAUTISTA ON THE RIO GRANDE, SAINT-DENIS FELL IN LOVE.

Oh, wonderous one, where have you been all my life?

Waiting for you to show up, my prince.

CONDUCTED TO MEXICO CITY, SAINT-DENIS WAS QUESTIONED CLOSELY AND GAVE THE RIGHT ANSWERS

All these Indians want the missionaries to return.

AFRAID THAT OTHER BOLD FRENCHMEN WOULD FOLLOW SAINT-DENIS'S TRACKS, SPAIN DECIDED TO REOCCUPY EAST TEXAS.

This time we'll leave not only priests but soldiers too.

SAN ANTONIO WAS FOUNDED IN 1718 AS A WAY-STATION ON THE ROAD BACK TO NACOGDOCHES.

This'll be a big city someday.

You think so?

THREE YEARS LATER A NEW GOVERNOR, THE MARQUES DE AGUAYO, EXTENDED THE KING'S HIGHWAY ON EASTWARD TO THE LOUISIANA BORDER, WHERE HE BUILT A STRONG FORT.

We can keep an eye on those crafty Frenchmen from here.

THIS PRESIDIO AT LOS ADAES (PRESENT ROBELINE, LA.) WAS THE CAPITAL OF TEXAS FOR FIFTY YEARS AND THE END OF THE LINE FOR PEOPLE TRAVELING UP THE CAMINO REAL FROM MEXICO.

Yeah, but nobody ever shows up.

IN 1731 THE KING SENT A FEW FAMILIES FROM THE CANARY ISLANDS TO SETTLE IN TEXAS. THEY STOPPED IN SAN ANTONIO AND FOUNDED A VILLA (TOWN) NEXT TO THE PRESIDIO.

This is the middle of nowhere.

THE FRANCISCAN MISSIONARIES HAD THEIR GREATEST SUCCESS AT SAN ANTONIO, WHERE FIVE MISSIONS FLOURISHED.

THEY TAUGHT THEIR INDIAN CONVERTS HOW TO RAISE CATTLE.

Now people will know who this calf belongs to—you!

THE MISSION VAQUEROS (COWBOYS) KEPT THEIR ESTABLISHMENTS SUPPLIED WITH BEEF.

Hiyah!

THEIR HERDS INCREASED RAPIDLY AND SOON WERE SO LARGE THAT NOT ALL COULD BE BRANDED; THE OTHERS RAN WILD.

We need lots of pasture land 'cause we own lots of cows.

THE MISSIONARIES MARKED THEIR LANDS WITH BOUNDARY STONES SO RUSTLERS COULDN'T PLEAD IGNORANCE.

Our ranch runs this far down th' road, right, Father?

APACHES SOMETIMES RAIDED THE MISSION HERDS OF LIVESTOCK.

AFTER A PEACE TREATY WITH THE APACHES IN 1749, PRIVATE RANCHERS BEGAN TO COMPETE WITH THE MISSIONS.

My ranch is downriver, right next to the mission's pasture... heh heh

THE SPANIARDS PLACED A PRESIDIO AND MISSION FOR THE APACHES ON THE SAN SABA RIVER IN 1757.

IT CAUSED PROBLEMS WITH THE COMANCHES AND OTHER NATIONS OF THE NORTH.

You are sheltering our sworn enemies.

WHEN THE ATTACK CAME, THERE WERE FEW SURVIVORS.

TO PUNISH THESE TRIBES FOR DESTROYING THE MISSION, CAPT. PARRILLA MARCHED NORTH IN AUGUST 1759 WITH AN ARMY OF OVER 500 MEN—THE LARGEST EXPEDITION SINCE CORONADO'S DAY. WITH HIM RODE SOME APACHE ALLIES.

AT THE BRAZOS RIVER HE STRUCK A TONKAWA VILLAGE, TAKING MANY CAPTIVES.

NOT SATISFIED WITH THIS VICTORY PARRILLA PRESSED ON, 200 LEAGUES INTO NOWHERE.

BY MID-OCTOBER HE REACHED THE RED RIVER AND BEHELD A STARTLING SIGHT: NO LITTLE HIDE-COVERED CAMP BUT A REAL FORTRESS, SURROUNDED BY A MOAT AND FLYING THE FRENCH FLAG! NEARBY THE COMANCHES WERE CAMPED.

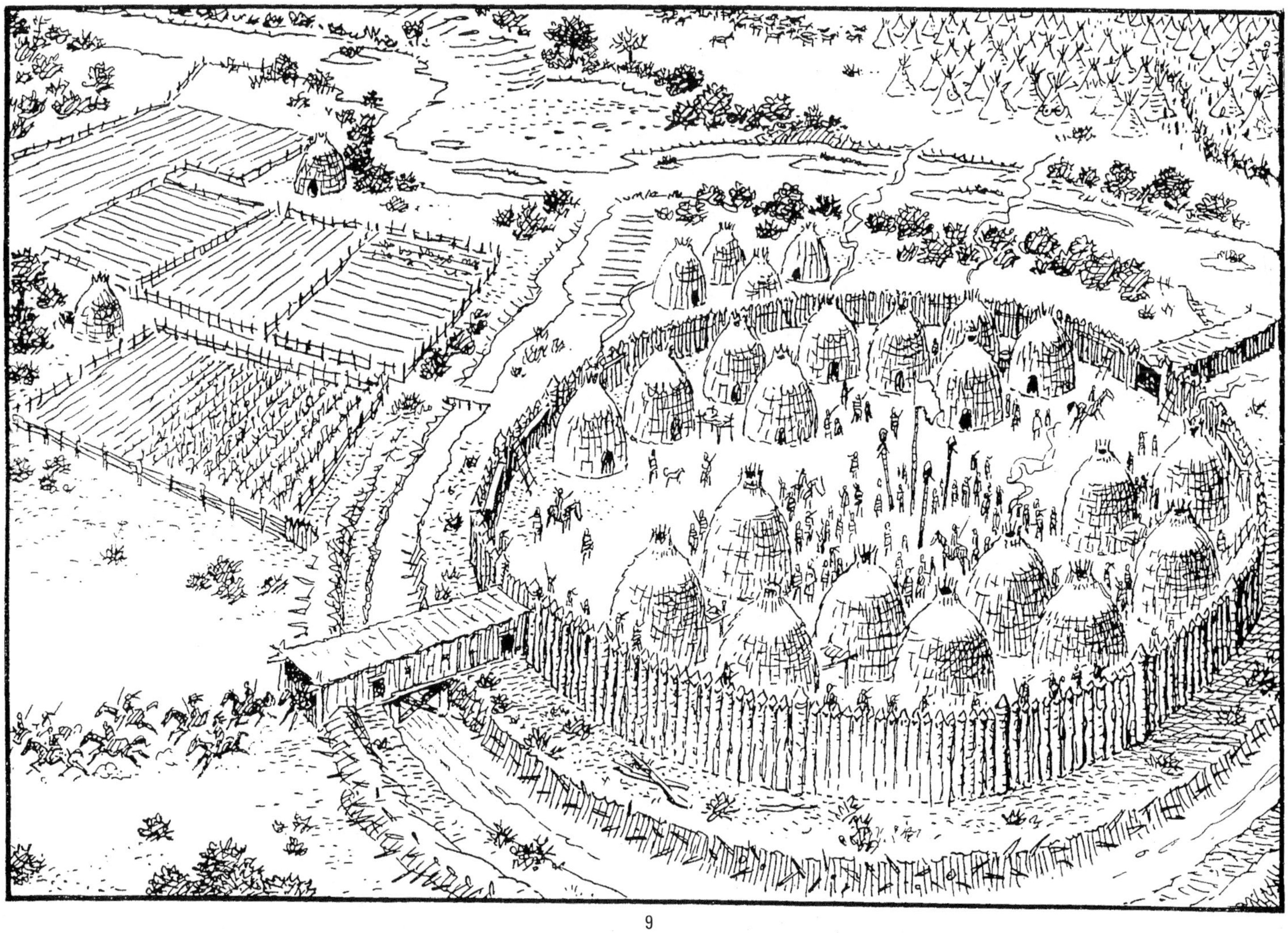

TIME AND AGAIN THE SPANISH SOLDIERS CHARGED THOSE STOUT WALLS, ALWAYS WITH THE SAME RESULT.

WICHITA WARRIORS RAINED DEATH DOWN ON THEM WHILE DRUMS AND FIFES PLAYED MERRILY.

THE SPANIARDS WERE FLUNG BACK, AND ONLY DARKNESS SAVED THEM FROM BEING WIPED OUT.

Back men, into the woods!

EMBOLDENED BY THIS VICTORY, THE COMANCHES PUSHED THE APACHES SOUTH, OUT OF THEIR BISON RANGE

CONSTANT INDIAN RAIDS KEPT TEXAS FROM DEVELOPING IN THE COLONIAL ERA.

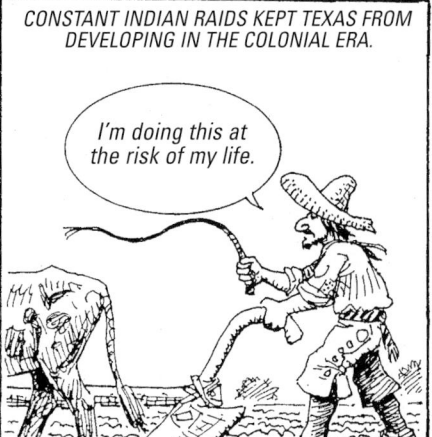

I'm doing this at the risk of my life.

AFTER SPAIN DECLARED WAR AGAINST ENGLAND IN 1779, THE RANCHERS OF TEXAS WERE ALLOWED TO TAKE HERDS OF CATTLE TO LOUISIANA.

Look out Opelousas, here we come.

THIS TRADE WAS HARD TO STOP IN LATER YEARS, AND SMUGGLING BECAME COMMON.

Somebody took a big herd through here last night.

DENIED LEGAL TRADE WITH LOUISIANA, THE CITIZENS OF TEXAS HAD TO TRAVEL THE LONG AND DANGEROUS ROUTE TO SALTILLO.

It takes a month to get there from San Antonio.

GOODS AT SALTILLO WERE SCARCE AND VERY EXPENSIVE, COMPARED TO THOSE AVAILABLE IN LOUISIANA.

Oh my achin' feet.

MEANWHILE, THE HERDS OF WILD HORSES MULTIPLIED IN TEXAS, ATTRACTING AMERICANS LIKE PHILIP NOLAN.

Horses bring a lot of money in Natchez and New Orleans these days.

NOLAN WAS SURROUNDED BY SPANISH TROOPS AT A HORSE CORRAL NEAR THE BRAZOS RIVER, AND A BATTLE ENSUED IN WHICH HE WAS KILLED.

NOLAN'S DEATH IN 1801 DIDN'T DO MUCH TO STEM THE FLOW OF AMERICANS PUSHING WESTWARD.

That's the end of that!

That's what you think.

NOLAN'S MEN WERE MADE PRISONERS AND SENT TO CHIHUAHUA. ONE OF THEM WAS YOUNG PETER ELLIS BEAN.

They haven't heard the last of me.

THE LOUISIANA PURCHASE OF 1803 MADE THE SPANIARDS EVEN MORE ANXIOUS ABOUT PROTECTING THEIR EXPOSED TEXAS FRONTIER.

Jefferson claims that Louisiana goes all the way to the Rio Grande.

What?! That's outrageous!

WAR ALMOST BROKE OUT BECAUSE SPAIN AND THE UNITED STATES COULDN'T AGREE ON THEIR NEW BOUNDARY LINE.

You're trespassing!

Get off our land!

SABINE RIVER

A DEAL WAS STRUCK BETWEEN OPPOSING GENERALS IN 1806.

No use of us fighting.

I couldn't agree more.

EVERYTHING BETWEEN THE RED RIVER AND THE SABINE WAS DECLARED A NEUTRAL GROUND, OR NO-MAN'S LAND, UNTIL DIPLOMATS COULD SETTLE THE QUESTION. TRAVEL BECAME DANGEROUS.

Your money or your life!

IN RESPONSE TO THE THREAT TWO NEW SETTLEMENTS WERE FOUNDED ON THE CAMINO REAL—AT THE SAN MARCOS AND TRINITY RIVER CROSSINGS. IT WAS TOO LITTLE, TOO LATE.

If we don't occupy Texas the Americans will.

THE COMANCHES RAN THE SETTLERS OUT OF SAN MARCOS DE NEVE, AND TRINIDAD DE SALCEDO NEVER AMOUNTED TO MUCH.

We should've stayed home.

SEVERAL YEARS LATER AN ARMY OF FILIBUSTERS RODE INTO NACOGDOCHES FROM LOUISIANA.

Where's th' Spaniards?

They hightailed it to San Antone.

GUTIERREZ AND MAGEE, THE EXPEDITION'S LEADERS, DECLARED TEXAS A REPUBLIC WHEN THEY REACHED THE DESERTED TRINITY OUTPOST.

Long live the Republic of the North.

NEXT THEY TOOK LA BAHIA (GOLIAD) AND HEADED FOR OLD SAN ANTONIO.

This is a piece of cake.

THE MURDER OF GOV. SALCEDO AND HIS OFFICERS TURNED THE AMERICAN VOLUNTEERS AGAINST GUTIERREZ. HE WAS REPLACED BY TOLEDO.

Killing prisoners of war is bad business.

BUT A SPANISH ARMY UNDER GEN. JOAQUIN DE ARREDONDO QUICKLY MARCHED UP FROM LAREDO.

I'll teach them a lesson they won't forget.

TOLEDO LED HIS TROOPS SOUTH TO MEET THEM.

We need a victory bad.

HIS CANNON GOT STUCK IN DEEP SAND BEFORE REACHING THE BATTLEFIELD.

Push—our artillery is essential!

AT A BATTLE BELOW THE MEDINA RIVER ARREDONDO DEALT THE REBELS A SMASHING BLOW.

We're beat, boys— let's head for Louisiana!

12

MOST WHO TRIED TO ESCAPE WERE CUT DOWN, OVER 600 OF THEM.

ONE OF ARREDONDO'S OFFICERS, COL. IGNACIO ELIZONDO, CHASED THE SURVIVORS UP THE CAMINO REAL TO THE TRINITY RIVER.

That settles that!

Maybe so, maybe no...

EXECUTIONS WERE FREQUENT FOR THOSE LEFT BEHIND.

AFTER ARREDONDO'S PURGE, TEXAS WAS A WASTELAND FOR YEARS.

Things gotta get better.

They can't get much worse.

DR. JAMES LONG LED ANOTHER FILIBUSTER RAID ON TEXAS, MOSTLY TO GIVE LAND TO HIS FOLLOWERS.

Down with tyranny!

HE TRIED TO ENLIST THE HELP OF PIRATE JEAN LAFFITE ON GALVESTON ISLAND.

You can raid Spanish ships with our government's okay.

BUT JEAN AND HIS BROTHER PIERRE KEPT THE SPANIARDS POSTED ON LONG'S VENTURE.

String them along till we learn their plans.

RUN OUT IN 1819, DR. LONG CAME BACK AGAIN THE NEXT YEAR. HE SET UP CAMP ON GALVESTON BAY.

We'll wait for more men to arrive.

NONE CAME SO HE ATTACKED AND TOOK GOLIAD WITH LESS THAN THIRTY MEN BUT WAS SOON FORCED TO SURRENDER.

We're freedom fighters like yourself.

LONG AND HIS MEN WERE SENT TO MEXICO CITY WHERE HE WAS KILLED UNDER MYSTERIOUS CIRCUMSTANCES.

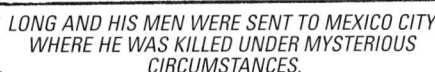

HIS WIFE, JANE LONG, WAITED FOR WORD ON THE FATE OF HER HUSBAND.

They say I'm a widow but I don't believe it.

IN 1820 AN AMERICAN NAMED MOSES AUSTIN HEADED TO SAN ANTONIO FROM MISSOURI WITH HOPES OF SETTLING THREE HUNDRED FAMILIES IN TEXAS.

I'll make a fresh start.

IN VIEW OF ALL THE RECENT TROUBLE WITH ANGLO ADVENTURERS, GOV. MARTINEZ TOLD AUSTIN TO GET OUT OF TOWN.

American colonists? That's the last thing we need.

BUT AUSTIN BUMPED INTO AN OLD ACQUAINTANCE ON MAIN PLAZA.

Why Moses Austin, what brings you here?

Why Baron de Bastrop, this is a small world.

BASTROP HAD PULL, SO AUSTIN GOT ANOTHER HEARING.

He's a loyal citizen and has developed lead mines in our territory.

Well, that changes things.

PASAPORTE.

AUSTIN'S PETITION TO BE AN EMPRESARIO (COLONIZATION AGENT) WAS ACCEPTED.

C'mon Richmond. We must sign up families back home.

THE TRIP BACK TO MISSOURI BROKE AUSTIN'S HEALTH.

Tell Stephen...to carry on...

WHEN MOSES DIED, THE COLONIZATION CONTRACT HE HAD OBTAINED FROM SPANISH AUTHORITIES PASSED TO HIS SON STEPHEN.

Father was right—this is a grand place.

STEPHEN TOURED TEXAS AND DECIDED TO LOCATE HIS COLONY BETWEEN THE LAVACA AND SAN JACINTO RIVERS.

This soil on the Brazos is the richest I've seen.

MEXICO GAINED ITS INDEPENDENCE FROM SPAIN IN 1821 SO AUSTIN HAD TO GET HIS FATHER'S GRANT APPROVED BY THE NEW GOVERNMENT.

My colonists are already arriving.

ON THE TRIP SOUTH HE AND HIS COMPANIONS WERE ATTACKED BY COMANCHES.

Hey, what's the big idea?

Our goose is cooked.

THINGS LOOKED BAD UNTIL THE INDIANS LEARNED THAT AUSTIN WAS NOT MEXICAN.

You Americans can go in peace. Americans are friends. Our war is with Mexicans.

Thanks. I'll remember that.

WHEN AUSTIN REACHED THE MEXICAN CAPITAL, GEN. AGUSTIN DE ITURBIDE WAS RULING THE COUNTRY AS EMPEROR.

THE EMPIRE FELL SHORTLY AFTER AUSTIN GAINED ITURBIDE'S APPROVAL, SO HIS RETURN TO TEXAS WAS DELAYED.

IT WAS NOT UNTIL APRIL 1823 THAT AUSTIN WAS ABLE TO LEAVE MEXICO CITY WITH ALL THE NECESSARY PAPERWORK TO BE AN EMPRESARIO.

TIMES WERE TOUGH FOR THE EARLY COLONISTS OF AUSTIN'S GRANT.

FORTUNATELY THERE WAS PLENTY OF WILD GAME.

THE LAND HAD TO BE CLEARED BEFORE CROPS COULD BE PLANTED AND HARVESTED. DROUGHT WAS SOMETIMES A PROBLEM.

BUT SETTLERS SWARMED IN, TOWNS WERE FORMED, AND CASH CROPS LIKE COTTON WERE SOON BEING PRODUCED.

MEXICO'S LIBERAL LAND POLICY ALLOWED OVER 4,000 ACRES TO A MAN WITH FAMILY, ALL AT PRICES MUCH CHEAPER THAN IN THE UNITED STATES.

APART FROM KARANKAWAS NEAR THE COAST, AUSTIN'S SETTLERS WERE NOT BOTHERED BY INDIANS.

THERE WERE OTHER EMPRESARIOS BESIDES AUSTIN. ONE WAS MARTIN DE LEON WHO FOUNDED THE TOWN OF VICTORIA.

We mostly raise cattle, horses & mules.

HIS COLONISTS SOMETIMES SUFFERED KARANKAWA RAIDS.

I hope they get what's coming to them.

ANOTHER WAS GREEN DEWITT, WHOSE COLONY WAS BELOW AUSTIN'S ON THE GUADALUPE RIVER.

Gonzales is our main town.

HADEN EDWARDS WAS AWARDED ALL THE TERRITORY AROUND NACOGDOCHES IN EAST TEXAS, BUT REFUSED TO HONOR PRIOR LAND CLAIMS AS HE WAS SUPPOSED TO.

Show me proof of title, or you're nothing but squatters and will have to get off— quick!

THIS CAUSED PROBLEMS FOR EDWARDS IN MEXICO CITY.

We don't need empresarios of this type

They're just rabble rousers.

NORTH OF NACOGDOCHES WERE MANY IMMIGRANT TRIBES FROM THE UNITED STATES, SUCH AS THE CHEROKEES UNDER CHIEF BOWL.

We're mostly farmers but do a lot of hunting too.

HE AND CHIEF RICHARD FIELDS GAINED PERMISSION TO STAY IN TEXAS BUT NOT CLEAR TITLE TO THEIR LANDS.

We'll let you know when a final decision is reached.

THE CHEROKEES LIVED IN COMPACT TOWNS AND PROSPERED, AS DID THEIR ALLIED TRIBES THE DELAWARES, SHAWNEES, AND KICKAPOOS.

JOHN DUNN HUNTER ARRIVED AMONG THESE INDIANS IN 1826 AND QUICKLY GAINED INFLUENCE OVER CHIEF FIELDS.

I couldn't get our land title nailed down, but maybe you'll have better luck.

HUNTER'S TRIP TO MEXICO CITY WAS UNSUCCESSFUL.

They'll only allow us to get land in individual tracts, not in a large communal grant like we want.

HIS NEWS CAUSED WAR DRUMS TO SOUND IN EAST TEXAS.

You'll either have to abandon your homes and return to the U.S. or prepare to defend yourselves against all comers!

CHIEF FIELDS WAS SO ANGRY HE WANTED TO FIGHT.

I am a Red Man of honor and won't be imposed on this way. We will hold our rich lands by force of arms!

Enough talk! It is time to act!

WHEN HIS CONTRACT WAS CANCELLED, HADEN EDWARDS AND HIS BROTHER BENJAMIN DECIDED TO DECLARE INDEPENDENCE.

Mexico won't let us manage our grant the way we see fit.

And now we stand to lose everything!

EDWARDS WAS COUNTING ON THE INDIANS FOR HELP IN HIS REBELLION.

Equal red and white stripes, symbolizing the union of our two peoples.

INDEPENDENCE
FREEDOM AND JUSTICE

LATER IN THE MONTH OF DECEMBER 1826 HUNTER AND FIELDS RETURNED TO NACOGDOCHES TO SIGN A FORMAL DECLARATION OF INDEPENDENCE.

The Red Man shall have all of Texas above the San Antonio Road, the White Man everything below.

LIVERY

PETER ELLIS BEAN, A SURVIVOR OF NOLAN'S EXPEDITION AND NOW AN INDIAN AGENT FOR MEXICO, TALKED THE CHEROKEES OUT OF JOINING EDWARDS.

Mexico will eventually give you lands—but not if you join in this rebellion.

WITH NO SUPPORT THE REBELS HAD TO FLEE TEXAS. FIELDS AND HUNTER WERE KILLED BEFORE THEY COULD ESCAPE ACROSS THE SABINE.

C'mon boys! We'll regroup in the Neutral Ground!

EVEN THOUGH AUSTIN'S AND DEWITT'S SETTLERS REFUSED TO SUPPORT THIS FREDONIAN REBELLION, THE MEXICAN GOVERNMENT BECAME VERY SUSPICIOUS OF ITS FOREIGN COLONISTS.

These Anglos are getting too strong.

If we're not careful, they'll take Texas away from us.

We'll see about that!

IN 1828 MEXICO SENT GEN. MIER Y TERAN TO SEE IF TEXAS WAS IN DANGER OF BEING LOST.

Already the foreigners outnumber the native Mexicans 8 to 1.

HIS REPORT CAUSED THE GOVERNMENT IN 1830 TO PROHIBIT MORE IMMIGRATION FROM THE UNITED STATES. AUSTIN OPPOSED THE MEASURE.

This is a terrible law. We must change it.

THE TEXANS MET AT CONVENTIONS IN 1832 AND 1833 IN FAVOR OF SEPARATE STATEHOOD FROM COAHUILA.

These meetings are illegal under Mexican law.

AUSTIN WAS CHOSEN TO DELIVER THE PETITIONS TO MEXICO CITY.

There'll be an uprising unless you agree to what we want.

HE WAS THROWN INTO PRISON DURING THIS VISIT AND STAYED THERE ALL OF 1834.

How can Texas live under a system such as this?

THE TEXANS FEARED TO TAKE ANY ACTION WHILE AUSTIN'S LIFE WAS IN DANGER.

Maybe they'll let him go if we stay quiet.

NOTICIA

IN JUNE 1835 HOTHEAD WILLIAM B. TRAVIS FORCED THE SMALL GARRISON AT ANAHUAC, NEAR THE MOUTH OF THE TRINITY RIVER, TO LEAVE TEXAS. A CRISIS WAS BARELY AVOIDED.

Get going while you still have the chance.

Si señor. You win— for now.

AUSTIN WAS RELEASED SHORTLY THEREAFTER. CHANGED BY HIS TIME IN JAIL, HE SPOKE FOR ARMED RESISTANCE.

We must go it on our own.

WHEN MEXICO DEMANDED THAT GONZALES GIVE UP ITS CANNON, HOSTILITIES BEGAN ON OCTOBER 2.

COME AND TAKE IT

GEN. MARTIN PERFECTO DE COS REINFORCED SAN ANTONIO WITH TROOPS. HE MADE THE MISTAKE OF INSULTING ERASMO SEGUIN.

I won't have a man as postmaster whose son is an avowed revolutionary! Get out!!

gasp

THE TEXANS WERE ABOUT TO GIVE UP THEIR SIEGE AND GO HOME WHEN A MEXICAN OFFICER DEFECTED AND BROUGHT GOOD NEWS.

He says their morale is really bad—that we can take Bexar easy.

You hear that boys? Unpack those mules.

BENJAMIN MILAM CALLED FOR AN ATTACK.

Who'll go with Ol' Ben Milam into San Antone!

Now you're talking.

THE FIGHTING WENT STREET TO STREET, HOUSE TO HOUSE.

ALTHOUGH MILAM WAS KILLED, COS WAS FORCED TO SURRENDER.

HIS MEN WERE ALLOWED TO MARCH SOUTH UNDER PLEDGE THAT THEY WOULD NOT FIGHT AGAIN AGAINST TEXAS.

Santa Anna isn't going to like this

SAM HOUSTON WAS A GREAT FRIEND OF THE CHEROKEES AND LIVED WITH THEM IN TENNESSEE IN HIS YOUTH.

IN 1833 HE MOVED TO TEXAS, FRESH FROM EXPERIENCE WITH THESE SAME CHEROKEES IN WESTERN ARKANSAS.

They adopted me into the tribe.

FORT GIBSON

ACTIVE IN THE 1835 CONSULTATION FOR TEXAS TO ESTABLISH A SEPARATE STATE GOVERNMENT FROM COAHUILA, HE WAS ELECTED A MAJOR GENERAL OF THE THEN NONEXISTENT TEXAS ARMY.

We haven't declared our independence yet, but war is inevitable.

TRYING TO MAKE SURE THAT THE CHEROKEES DIDN'T TAKE THE MEXICAN SIDE, HOUSTON SIGNED A TREATY WITH CHIEF BOWL ON FEBRUARY 23, 1836.

Here's where the boundary line will run.

HOUSTON, ALTHOUGH NEUTRALIZING THE CHEROKEES IN THE COMING STRUGGLE, COULD NOT GAIN THEIR ACTIVE PARTICIPATION.

We just want to stay out of the blood-shed entirely.

Alright. That's good enough.

WORD SOON CAME THAT GEN. SANTA ANNA WAS MARCHING A LARGE ARMY NORTH TO RETAKE TEXAS, THOUGH NO ONE EXPECTED HIM TO MAKE IT SO SOON.

HE REACHED SAN ANTONIO ON THE SAME DAY THAT HOUSTON SIGNED HIS TREATY WITH THE CHEROKEES.

Rouse our men! Carry off everything you can to the Alamo, double-quick!

SANTA ANNA BEGAN A SIEGE OF THE ALAMO THAT LASTED THIRTEEN DAYS.

Bravo! Keep pounding the walls till they tumble down.

THIS CONSTANT BOMBARDMENT GAVE THE ALAMO DEFENDERS LITTLE CHANCE FOR SLEEP.

ONLY A FEW REINFORCEMENTS CAME ON MARCH 1.

See boys? It's still possible for help to reach us! If these 32 can make it in, so can Fannin's 332!

BUT NO MORE HELP ARRIVED, DESPITE TRAVIS'S PLEAS. THEIR SITUATION WAS BECOMING DESPERATE.

ONCE HE REALIZED THE SITUATION WAS HOPELESS, COL. TRAVIS GAVE HIS MEN A CHOICE.

Boys, we can either surrender and be shot, run and be cut down, or stand and sell our lives dearly!

As for me, I will not abandon my post and have resolved to die in these cold ditches.

Let my bones be a reproach to our fellow Texians for their neglect in our hour of need!

IT IS BELIEVED THAT TRAVIS DRAMATIZED THIS OFFER BY DRAWING A LINE IN THE SAND WITH HIS SWORD. MYTH OR NOT, THIS STORY HAS REFUSED TO DIE.

If any of you will stand beside me and fight until the last breath of life expires, let them cross this line!

Step over boys! Who will be the first?

AMONG THOSE STAYING TO THE END WERE JAMES BOWIE, WHO WAS SICK AND BEDRIDDEN, AND DAVID CROCKETT.

We might as well fight, for escape is well nigh impossible.

UNKNOWN TO TRAVIS AND HIS BRAVE MEN, TEXAS HAD DECLARED ITS INDEPENDENCE ON MARCH 2. TEJANOS FRANCISCO RUIZ AND JOSE ANTONIO NAVARRO WERE SIGNERS.

Steady, nephew. Your hand need not tremble for the cause of freedom.

True, but when Santa Anna sees what we've signed, it'll be our death warrant.

LED BY GEN. AMADOR ONE, THEN ANOTHER, MADE IT OVER THE WALL AT DAWN ON MARCH 6.

(AFTER FRAY)

TRAVIS, BESIDE HIS CANNON, WAS AN EARLY CASUALTY.

AFTER THE MEXICAN SOLDIERS STREAMED INTO THE COMPOUND, THE TEXAN DEFENDERS STOOD LITTLE CHANCE OF SURVIVAL.

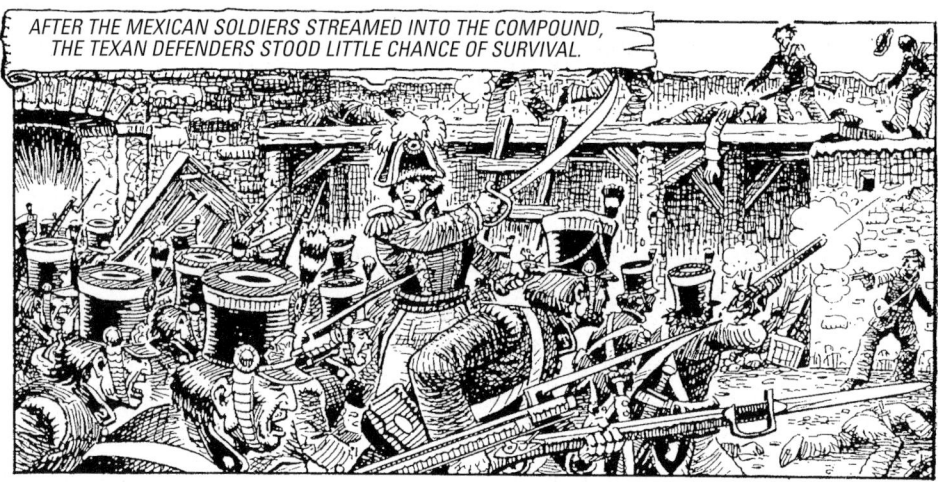

BOWIE AWAITED DEATH IN HIS SICKROOM.

From the sound of it, that door will open soon.

THE FATE OF CROCKETT IS STILL DEBATED. DID HE GO DOWN FIGHTING OR WAS HE CAPTURED AND EXECUTED?

Keep at it fellers. Ol' Gabriel ain't blowed his horn yet!

SUSANNA DICKINSON WAS RELEASED TO CARRY WORD OF THE MEXICAN VICTORY TO THE ANGLO SETTLEMENTS.

THUS BEGAN WHAT WAS KNOWN AS THE RUNAWAY SCRAPE. WOMEN AND CHILDREN HASTENED TO ESCAPE SANTA ANNA'S ARMY.

Won't be safe until we're over th' Sabine.

THIS MEXICAN VICTORY WAS FOLLOWED BY ANOTHER AT GOLIAD, WHERE JAMES FANNIN DELAYED UNTIL IT WAS TOO LATE TO WITHDRAW SAFELY.

My post at Goliad is more critical to the defense of Texas than the Alamo!

DEFEATED NEAR COLETO CREEK, FANNIN'S CAPTURED FORCE OF ALMOST 400 MEN WAS EXECUTED BY SANTA ANNA'S ORDER.

SANTA ANNA PURSUED HOUSTON'S RETREATING ARMY TO THE BRAZOS, WHERE HE MADE A FATEFUL DECISION.

If we capture the rebel government the war will be over.

Good thinking Your Excellency.

HOUSTON LEARNED THAT SANTA ANNA WAS RACING AHEAD OF HIS MAIN ARMY WITH A SMALL FORCE.

We've finally got him where we want him. Let's ride!!

THE TEXANS MET SANTA ANNA'S VANGUARD AT SAN JACINTO ON APRIL 21, SCORING A COMPLETE VICTORY.

Remember the Alamo! Remember Goliad!!

JUAN SEGUIN LED A COMPANY OF TEJANOS IN THE BATTLE, SHOUTING THE SAME CRY.

RECUERDEN EL ALAMO!

BUT SANTA ANNA WAS CAPTURED THE NEXT DAY. HE ORDERED HIS 4,000-MAN ARMY TO LEAVE TEXAS.

SAM HOUSTON, SUFFERING FROM A GUNSHOT WOUND IN HIS ANKLE, SPENT AN UNEASY NIGHT FEARING HIS PREY HAD ELUDED HIM.

Boys, we've got to catch Santa Anna or face another fight.

He says they'll go if he tells them to.

THE RETREAT CONTINUED TO THE RIO GRANDE IN BAD WEATHER, THUS ASSURING TEXAS INDEPENDENCE.

For the time being anyway.

SAM HOUSTON, THE HERO OF SAN JACINTO, WAS ELECTED THE FIRST PRESIDENT OF THE REPUBLIC OF TEXAS.

We face some hard times and must conserve our energy.

LATER THAT YEAR STEPHEN F. AUSTIN, THE FATHER OF TEXAS, DIED AT AGE 43.

Texas is recognized. Did you see it in the papers?

BUT THE UNITED STATES WOULDN'T RECOGNIZE THE INDEPENDENCE OF TEXAS OR ADMIT HER TO THE UNION.

We must wait and see if a free Texas can endure.

HOUSTON WANTED TO AVOID MORE FIGHTING WITH MEXICO AND KEEP PEACE WITH THE INDIANS.

Let's make treaties with them and not attack Mexico till we're attacked.

THE CHEROKEES WERE QUIET, BUT COMANCHES KEPT UP THEIR ATTACKS ON EXPOSED SETTLEMENTS LIKE PARKER'S FORT.

We'll use a white flag to get in. That always works.

AFTER THE ATTACK BEGAN LUCY PARKER TRIED TO ESCAPE WITH HER FOUR YOUNG CHILDREN.

Cynthia!! Hurry children, run!

MOUNTED WARRIORS FORCED HER TO HOIST CYNTHIA AND JOHN UP BEHIND THEM.

Momma, momma!

Please don't take my babies...

THUS CYNTHIA ANN PARKER WAS SWEPT AWAY TO BE RAISED AS A COMANCHE, HER BROTHER JOHN AS WELL.

RAIDS LIKE THIS, WITH THE LOSS OF WOMEN AND CHILDREN AS CAPTIVES, MADE THE TEXANS HATE THE COMANCHES.

Momma always said crying doesn't help...sniff.

AT THE END OF 1837 THE TEXAS SENATE REFUSED TO RATIFY HOUSTON'S TREATY WITH THE CHEROKEES.

Don't worry chief, just a temporary setback.

THIS MADE BOWL LISTEN TO MEXICAN PROMISES OF A RECONQUEST OF TEXAS.

We want you to take the field immediately. Here's powder, lead, and tobacco for your men!

A FEW MEXICAN CITIZENS OF NACOGDOCHES, LED BY VICENTE CORDOVA, PROMOTED THIS UNREST.

Gen. Filisola's organizing a big campaign down at Matamoros right now. We've got to be ready...

BUT GEN. THOMAS RUSK CHASED THESE MEXICAN AGENTS OUT OF BOWL'S VILLAGE.

Do not allow these bad men to come into your nation.

KNOWING HOUSTON'S REGARD FOR THE CHEROKEES, AND BEING A FRIEND OF HIS, RUSK WAS IN A DIFFICULT SPOT.

General, settle this infernal question of whether it's peace or war with the Cherokees so we can get going!

IN MID-OCTOBER 1838 RUSK TRIED TO ATTACK A COMBINED KICKAPOO, MEXICAN, CADDO, COUSHATTA, AND KICHAI CAMP BUT WAS AMBUSHED BEFORE REACHING IT.

Pull back men. They are too well concealed.

MEANWHILE PRESIDENT HOUSTON ORDERED THE SURVEY OF CHEROKEE LANDS.

Rusk's troops won't attack you, long as you keep your young men out of this war.

DESPITE THESE TROUBLES, SETTLERS KEPT COMING TO TEXAS.

Where you folks from?

Missouri's th' latest place.

NACADOCH OR BUST

PORTS WERE OPENED AND MORE NEW ROADS LINKED THE INTERIOR TO THESE BUSTLING TRADE CENTERS ALONG THE GULF COAST.

Can we buy some fancy chocolate, Pa?

And a french harp for Ollie?

BORDEN DRY GOODS

WAR HERO JUAN SEGUIN SERVED AS A SENATOR FROM SAN ANTONIO. HE WORKED FOR THE RIGHTS OF HIS PEOPLE.

EARLY TEXAS RANGERS RENAMED THEIR TOWN OF WALNUT SPRINGS ON THE GUADALUPE RIVER FOR HIM.

ANOTHER WAR HERO, MIRABEAU LAMAR, BECAME THE SECOND PRESIDENT OF THE REPUBLIC OF TEXAS AT THE END OF 1838.

LAMAR'S FIRST POLICY STATEMENT LET TEXANS KNOW THE COURSE HE INTENDED TO PURSUE.

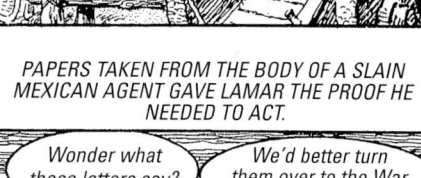

PAPERS TAKEN FROM THE BODY OF A SLAIN MEXICAN AGENT GAVE LAMAR THE PROOF HE NEEDED TO ACT.

PRESIDENT LAMAR GAVE CHIEF BOWL AN ULTIMATUM.

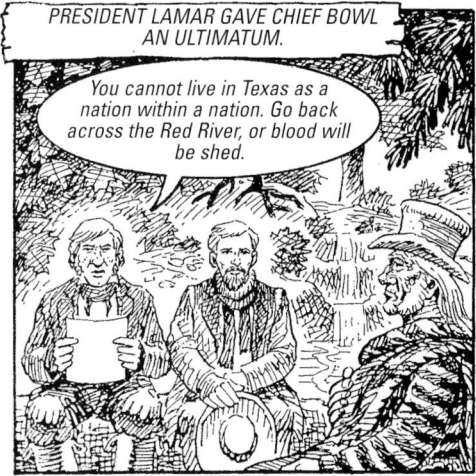

THE CHIEF STALLED ON SIGNING A TREATY FOR REMOVAL.

RUSK'S ARMY ADVANCED ON BOWL'S VILLAGE, ONLY TO FIND IT EMPTY.

THE TEXANS PURSUED AND DROVE THE CHEROKEES OUT OF TEXAS, JUST AS LAMAR HAD PROMISED WHEN ELECTED AS PRESIDENT.

CHIEF BOWL, SAM HOUSTON'S FRIEND, WAS KILLED IN THE BATTLE.

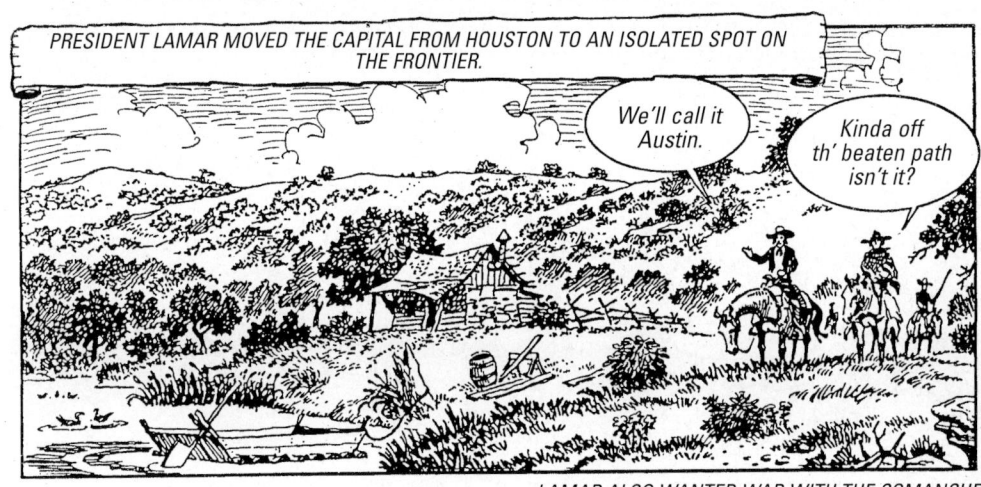

PRESIDENT LAMAR MOVED THE CAPITAL FROM HOUSTON TO AN ISOLATED SPOT ON THE FRONTIER.

We'll call it Austin.

Kinda off th' beaten path isn't it?

LAMAR WAS A STRONG BELIEVER IN THE BENEFITS OF EDUCATION.

Let's set aside public land to fund good schools.

SAM HOUSTON, AS A REPRESENTATIVE IN THE TEXAS HOUSE, OPPOSED MANY OF LAMAR'S MEASURES—ESPECIALLY THOSE CONCERNING INDIANS.

His war on the Cherokees was unjustified.

LAMAR ALSO WANTED WAR WITH THE COMANCHES. TWELVE CHIEFS WERE KILLED IN 1840 AT SAN ANTONIO'S COUNCIL HOUSE WHEN THEY CAME FOR PEACE TALKS BUT FAILED TO DELIVER THEIR WHITE CAPTIVES.

Not a single one left alive.

A WOMAN WAS RELEASED TO CARRY BACK THE NEWS.

Tell your tribe we want our prisoners brought in.

THE COMANCHES RETALIATED BY RAIDING ALL THE WAY TO THE COAST, DESTROYING THE PORT OF LINNVILLE AND PICKING THE COUNTRY CLEAN.

Ahh...just like old times.

ALTHOUGH RANGERS TRACKED THE RAIDERS AND RECOVERED MUCH OF THEIR BOOTY, THIS RUNNING FIGHT REVEALED A PROBLEM.

We need better weapons for this kind of war.

THE ONLY REAL WAY TO FIGHT THE INDIANS WAS FROM HORSEBACK, BUT WHEN IT CAME TO MOUNTED WARFARE, NO ONE WAS SUPERIOR TO THE WILD COMANCHES.

Hii Yiii!

Go for th' gusto!

THE TEXANS' MUZZLE LOADERS WERE CLUMSY AFFAIRS AND COULDN'T BE FIRED EFFECTIVELY OR RELOADED AT A GALLOP.

Oops, there went my ramrod.

THIS MEANT THE RANGERS HAD TO DISMOUNT AND FIRE ONE VOLLEY, AFTER WHICH THE CIRCLING INDIANS SWOOPED IN TO ATTACK WHILE THE TEXANS WERE DESPERATELY TRYING TO RELOAD.

Brace yourself boys. Here they come!

Ball...did I put th' ball in before or???

Powder's lumpy...

Come back here.

THUS THE RANGERS HAD TO WAGE A STRICTLY DEFENSIVE WAR AND COULDN'T DO MUCH DAMAGE TO THE HARD-RIDING COMANCHES, WHO REMAINED MASTERS OF THE PLAINS AND HILL COUNTRY.

Ouch!

You fellers need to try some modern weapons—bows 'n arrows!

ALL THIS BEGAN TO CHANGE IN 1839 WHEN A SWEDISH TRADER NAMED SWANTE SWENSON CARRIED BACK TO TEXAS A DOZEN NEW-FANGLED PISTOLS INVENTED BY SAMUEL COLT.

These things oughta sell like hotcakes.

A FRIEND OF PRESIDENT LAMAR'S SHOWED HIM THE 5-SHOOTERS ON BEHALF OF THE STARVING INVENTOR.

Five shots! Hmm..now that's a concept whose time has come.

LAMAR SENT TWO OF THE REVOLVERS TO A YOUNG RANGER NAMED JACK HAYS.

Boys, this is what we've been waiting for.

BUT HAYS WAS FRUSTRATED IN HIS ATTEMPT TO GET COLTS FOR HIS RANGERS. THE FIRST ORDER OF PISTOLS AND RIFLES WENT TO LAMAR'S BRASH NEW NAVY IN SUPPORT OF YUCATAN'S FREEDOM FROM MEXICO.

Eat lead, you lubbers!

ONLY A FEW PISTOLS MADE THEIR WAY INTO RANGER HANDS FROM PRIVATE SOURCES LIKE SWENSON.

They're expensive but worth it.

GOODS

DURING LAMAR'S TERM OF OFFICE REVOLTS BROKE OUT IN NORTHERN MEXICO IN WHICH THE FEDERALIST REBELS WERE ANXIOUS TO GAIN TEXAN SUPPORT.

Viva Canales

Viva Arista

ANTONIO CANALES, A PROMINENT CITIZEN OF TAMAULIPAS, WAS THE MILITARY LEADER OF THIS REBELLION.

We want to set up our own republic along the Rio Grande.

PRESIDENT LAMAR STAYED NEUTRAL BUT ALLOWED THE REBELS TO RECRUIT IN TEXAS.

Anything that distracts Mexico is good for us.

MANY TEXANS ENLISTED IN THESE CAMPAIGNS, ESPECIALLY MEN ACCUSTOMED TO FIGHTING INDIANS AND BANDITS ON THE FRONTIER.

Welcome compañeros! You come to help us win our freedom, no?

Si, si, amigo. You betcha..

DEEP IN MEXICO THE TEXANS FOUND THAT NEITHER THE FEDERALISTS NOR THE CENTRALISTS CARED MUCH FOR THEM.

Looks like we'll have to fight our way to the border, boys. They're both shooting at us!

JUAN SEGUIN RESIGNED AS SENATOR TO LEAD A COMPANY OF VOLUNTEERS IN THIS REVOLT. UPON REACHING THE RIO GRANDE, HE LEARNED THAT THE SITUATION HAD CHANGED.

It's getting sticky down there Juan. Canales has made peace with Arista's troops.

We were lucky to get back with our skins!

IN 1841 LAMAR BACKED AN EXPEDITION TO SANTA FE, NEW MEXICO.

Trade through Santa Fe is very rich, and we need to control it.

We'll offer them Texas citizenship.

HE PICKED JOSE ANTONIO NAVARRO AS ONE OF THE MEN TO HEAD HIS GRANDIOSE SCHEME.

I have reservations about this, Mr. President..

Nonsense!! You're the only man qualified for the job. It's your patriotic duty to Texas!

LAMAR'S AGENTS FOOLISHLY WARNED THE NEW MEXICANS IN AN OPEN LETTER THAT TEXANS WERE ON THE WAY

We tore down all we found in the plaza.

Hmph! Let them come. We'll give 'um a hot reception!

IT WAS A FIASCO, AND THE TEXANS WERE CAPTURED BEFORE EVEN REACHING SANTA FE. ONE OF THEIR COMRADES TALKED THEM INTO SURRENDERING THEIR WEAPONS.

Believe me boys, giving up your guns is only a formality—customary procedure for the Santa Fe trade.

?!

ALL THE TEXAN PRISONERS ENDURED GREAT SUFFERING, BUT NAVARRO—HATED BY SANTA ANNA BECAUSE HE HAD SIGNED THE DECLARATION OF INDEPENDENCE FROM MEXICO—SUFFERED WORST OF ALL.

I have sworn to be a Texan, and I will remain one!

TEXAS WAS DEEP IN DEBT BY THE TIME LAMAR'S TERM ENDED AND HOUSTON BECAME PRESIDENT ONCE AGAIN.

Not a dollar in the treasury and our credit's no good.

HE REVERSED LAMAR'S INDIAN POLICY AND TRIED TO MAKE TREATIES WITH THE DIFFERENT TRIBES.

It's much cheaper and more humane to purchase their friendship than it is to fight them.

AGENTS AND TRADERS SUCH AS JESSE CHISHOLM WERE SENT OUT TO MEND LAMAR'S DAMAGE WITH THE WILD TRIBES, ESPECIALLY THE FIERCE COMANCHES.

I bring gifts for you. Let's hold a big peace talk.

MEXICO LAUNCHED AN ATTACK ON SAN ANTONIO EARLY IN 1842.

I hereby declare you to be citizens of Mexico— again!

A LARGER INVASION CAME LATER THAT YEAR, BUT MATHEW OLD PAINT CALDWELL RALLIED RESISTANCE.

Keep cool and remember— we fight for liberty and our insulted country!

GEN. ADRIAN WOLL OCCUPIED THE CITY FOR TEN DAYS BEFORE RETREATING SOUTH WITH 58 PROMINENT CITIZENS AS PRISONERS OF WAR. SAM MAVERICK WAS AMONG THEM.

SAM HOUSTON WAS NEVER FOND OF THE EXPOSED LOCATION THAT MIRABEAU LAMAR HAD CHOSEN FOR THE REPUBLIC'S CAPITAL.

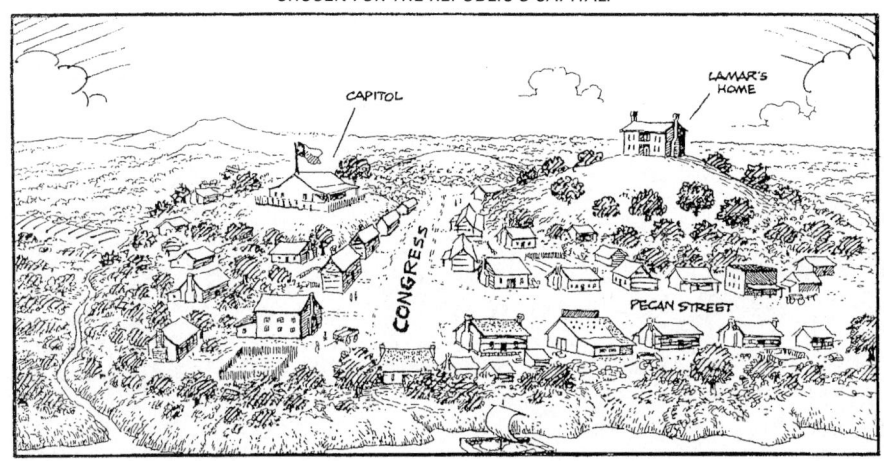

AS CHIEF EXECUTIVE HOUSTON DECIDED TO MOVE IT EAST, TOWARD THE ESTABLISHED SETTLEMENTS.

I'll use the Mexican threat as an excuse.

HIS ATTEMPT TO TAKE THE ARCHIVES OUT OF AUSTIN WAS THWARTED BY ANGELINA EBERLY, WHO FIRED OFF A CANNON TO ALERT THE CITIZENS.

Wake up! They're stealing the public papers!

THE TWO MEXICAN INVASIONS IN 1842 MADE WARLIKE TEXANS CALL FOR AN ARMED RESPONSE AGAINST THE BORDER TOWNS. IT ENDED IN DEFEAT AT MIER WITH MORE THAN 200 PRISONERS TAKEN.

We're in for it now, boys.

THE TEXANS BROKE THEIR WEAPONS SO THE MEXICANS COULDN'T CAPTURE AND USE THEM IN FUTURE BATTLES.

Quick now.

AN ESCAPE ATTEMPT LED BY EWEN CAMERON RESULTED IN THE BLACK BEAN EPISODE. SEVENTEEN MEN WHO DREW BLACK BEANS WERE EXECUTED.

CAMERON DREW A WHITE BEAN BUT WAS KILLED ANYWAY.

No blindfold. For the liberty of Texas I can look death in the face.

THE REST OF THE TEXAN PRISONERS JOINED THOSE TAKEN AT SANTA FE AND SAN ANTONIO.

poor devil

GAKKKK...

MEN WHO MANAGED TO ESCAPE BLAMED PRESIDENT HOUSTON FOR ABANDONING THEM IN THEIR HOUR OF NEED.

No Houston, I will not shake your hand.

Sorry you feel that way, Mr. Walker.

HOUSTON KEPT UP HIS EFFORTS FOR PEACE WITH THE INDIANS.

Chief Placido, this stew is mighty tasty.

Yeah, we like our dog meat boiled with herbs.

WITH LITTLE MONEY IN THE TREASURY, FRONTIER DEFENSE WAS LEFT TO RANGING COMPANIES LED BY MEN LIKE JACK HAYS.

Me and Jack's pa fought together at Horseshoe Bend!

EARLY IN 1844 HOUSTON GAVE HAYS THE COLT PISTOLS FORMERLY USED BY LAMAR'S NAVY.

Better late than never, eh son?

Hit them before they can reload. Now!!

THAT JUNE HAYS'S MEN GOT THEIR CHANCE IN THE PEDERNALES HILLS. THEY ASTOUNDED A COMANCHE WAR PARTY, LONG ACCUSTOMED TO A FOE WITH ONLY ONE ROUND OF FIREPOWER.

THIS BATTLE MARKED A TURNING POINT IN INDIAN WARFARE ON THE FRONTIER. FOR THE FIRST TIME THE TEXANS HELD THE ADVANTAGE IN A RUNNING FIGHT.

Throw down your rifles and mount up!

BEFORE LONG, THE COMANCHES CAME TO FEAR THE MEN WITH A SHOT FOR EACH FINGER, AND THEIR POWER BEGAN TO STEADILY DECLINE.

Keep on pushing 'um boys. Don't let up!

THANKS TO THIS VICTORY, CHIEF BUFFALO HUMP AGREED TO HAVE A PEACE COUNCIL WITH PRESIDENT HOUSTON IN OCTOBER 1844.

My peace with the Comanches held until a Bad Chief took my place and made war on your people at San Antonio.

BUFFALO HUMP WAS PLEASED, BUT HE DEMANDED THAT A LINE BE DRAWN TO MARK COMANCHE LANDS.

We must be able to follow the buffalo on their winter migration south.

UNABLE TO DECIDE ON WHERE A DIVISION LINE WOULD RUN, THEY SIGNED A PEACE TREATY WITHOUT THIS PROVISION.

We will rub out that part and go on as before, until we can agree.

SCOUTS AND INTERPRETERS—MOST OF THEM DELAWARES OR SHAWNEES—SECURED PEACE WITH OTHER TRIBES SUCH AS THE WICHITAS.

Trading posts will be established near your country so that you lack in nothing.

HOUSTON'S SUCCESSOR AS PRESIDENT, ANSON JONES, CONTINUED THIS PEACEFUL APPROACH.

The new president has sent us to say that he is still anxious to live in harmony with his red brothers on the plains.

JOSE ANTONIO NAVARRO ESCAPED FROM PRISON BARELY IN TIME TO ATTEND THE CONVENTION THAT DECIDED FOR ANNEXATION TO THE UNITED STATES IN 1845.

Looks like I'm the only Tejano here.

HE SPOKE AGAINST THE WORD "WHITE" BEING WRITTEN IN THE STATE CONSTITUTION AS A VOTER QUALIFICATION.

Some election judge might use it as an excuse to keep my people from voting.

THE VOTERS OF TEXAS GAVE THEIR APPROVAL TO ANNEXATION, AND ON FEBRUARY 19, 1846, ANSON JONES PROCLAIMED THAT THE REPUBLIC OF TEXAS WAS NO MORE.

MEXICO'S REPRESENTATIVE IN WASHINGTON, JUAN ALMONTE, HAD ALREADY TOLD THE U.S. GOVERNMENT THAT ANNEXATION WOULD MEAN WAR.

Texas has always belonged to Mexico!

U.S. TROOPS UNDER GEN. ZACHARY TAYLOR MOVED SOUTH FROM THEIR BASE AT CORPUS CHRISTI, ANTICIPATING MEXICO'S RESPONSE.

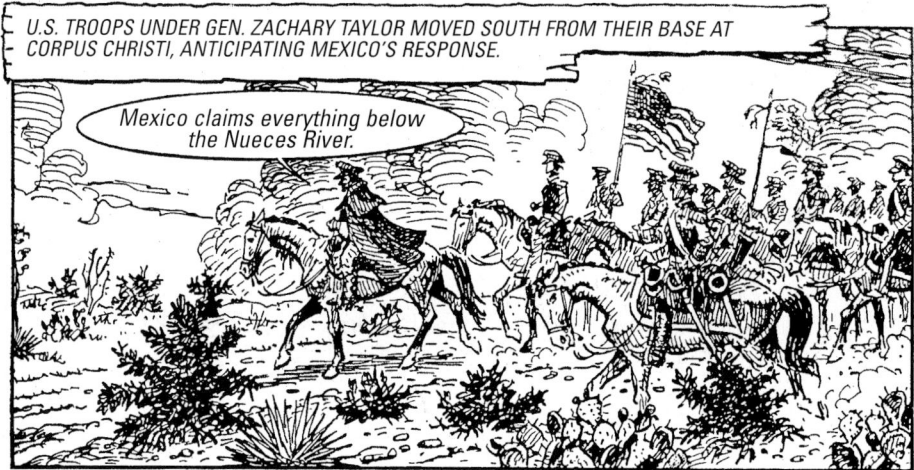

Mexico claims everything below the Nueces River.

THE RESPONSE CAME QUICKLY AT PALO ALTO AND RESACA DE LA PALMA, JUST ABOVE MATAMOROS, BUT TAYLOR'S TROOPS PUT GEN. ARISTA AND THE MEXICAN ARMY TO FLIGHT.

GEN. TAYLOR WAS EAGER TO HAVE MORE TEXANS IN HIS ARMY AS HE PLANNED OPERATIONS AGAINST MONTERREY.

Nobody can tell me what's happening better than these rangers from Texas.

WHEN JACK HAYS, SAM WALKER, BEN MCCULLOCH, AND OTHER FORMER RANGERS JOINED TAYLOR'S ARMY THEY CARRIED THEIR COLTS WITH THEM.

AFTER THE SURRENDER OF MONTERREY, WALKER WENT TO SEE COLT IN NEW YORK WITH A WHITTLED MODEL OF A NEW PISTOL THE TEXANS WANTED.

Tell him to make it heavier so we can use it for a club when we run out of bullets.

COLT'S 5-SHOOTER HAD MET WITH LITTLE SUCCESS, APART FROM ITS POPULARITY IN TEXAS. HE WAS BANKRUPT AND LIVING IN POVERTY.

Captain Walker, you're on to something here... but selling the military brass on it is another matter entirely.

WALKER'S ORDER FOR A THOUSAND OF THE NEW 6-SHOOTERS PUT SAM COLT BACK IN BUSINESS.

Bless those Texans.

HE NAMED IT THE WALKER COLT, IN HONOR OF THE DASHING YOUNG WAR HERO WHO HAD HELPED HIM IMPROVE HIS DESIGN—AND CONVINCE THE U.S. ARMY TO BUY IT!

Don't worry. I'll see to it that you get your pistols.

Thanks, Mr. President.

COL. HAYS EQUIPPED ALL HIS TEXAN VOLUNTEERS WITH TWO OF THE HEFTY NEW 6-SHOOTERS WHEN THEY REACHED HIM AT VERACRUZ.

Don't lose them!! The Army's slow about replacements..

CAPT. WALKER WAS ARMED WITH A SPECIAL PRESENTATION BRACE WHEN HE FELL IN THE STORMING OF HUAMANTLA ON OCTOBER 9, 1847.

AFTER VICTORY IN THE MEXICAN WAR, TEXAS—AS PART OF THE UNION—ENTERED A PERIOD OF GROWTH AND STABILITY.

Cotton is king, and we raise lots of cotton.

RANCHERS BEGAN TO TRAIL HERDS TO OUTSIDE MARKETS.

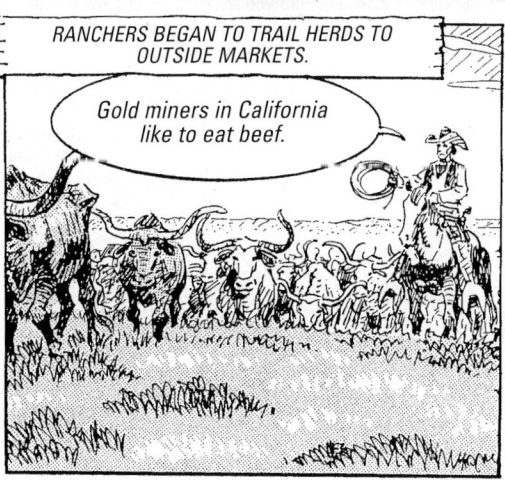

Gold miners in California like to eat beef.

SAM HOUSTON AND TOM RUSK SERVED AS SEN-ATORS FROM TEXAS, WORKING ON ISSUES LIKE THE COMPROMISE OF 1850.

This boundary settlement will allow Texas to pay off its debts.

A NEW STATE CAPITOL WAS BUILT IN THE EARLY 1850s AT AUSTIN.

Now this town will grow.

Wish we had a big school.

HAVING RETAINED CONTROL OVER ITS PUBLIC LANDS, TEXAS IN THE MID-1850s ESTABLISHED TWO SMALL RESERVATIONS FOR THE INDIANS.

Probably won't work but we'll give it a try.

ROBERT S. NEIGHBORS WAS APPOINTED AGENT TO TALK THE VARIOUS TRIBES INTO ACCEPTING RESERVATION LIFE.

Come on up to th' new Brazos Reserve— you'll be safe there.

NEIGHBORS WAS A BEAR OF A MAN, WELL-LIKED AND TRUSTED BY THE INDIANS BECAUSE HE SEEMED TO HAVE THEIR INTERESTS AT HEART.

THE PEACEFUL TRIBES MADE SOME PROGRESS IN THEIR NEW HOME. THE COMANCHES, HOWEVER, DID-N'T WANT TO SETTLE DOWN AND BECOME FARMERS.

These melons and squash look real good, wife.

AIDED BY CHIEF PLACIDO AND HIS TONKAWA WARRIORS, RANGER CAPTAIN JOHN S. RIP FORD DECIDED TO ATTACK THE COMANCHES ON THEIR HOME GROUND.

I don't like those wild Indians any better than you, Col. John.

THEY WON A BATTLE AGAINST THE NOTED CHIEF IRON JACKET IN 1858.

Hey Hey, you possum lovers, come out and fight Iron Jacket!!

IN ANOTHER BATTLE CYNTHIA ANN PARKER WAS RECAPTURED FROM THE COMANCHES.

I'll betcha this is the Parker girl we keep hearing about.

MARRIED TO CHIEF PETA NOCONA WITH THREE CHILDREN, SHE COULD NOT MAKE THE TRANSITION BACK TO LIFE WITH WHITE PEOPLE. THE DEATH OF HER LITTLE DAUGHTER TOPSANNAH CRUSHED HER SPIRIT.

Cynthia, eat something, honey...You'll starve yourself like this...

CYNTHIA ANN WASTED AWAY AND FINALLY DIED OF A BROKEN HEART, BUT HER SON QUANAH WENT ON TO BECOME A FAMOUS COMANCHE CHIEF.

Won't stir, won't eat, never smiles...I just don't know.

THE RESERVATION EXPERIMENT WAS A FAILURE, AND AGENT NEIGHBORS HAD TO TAKE THESE TRIBES TO OKLAHOMA (THEN CALLED INDIAN TERRITORY).

Couldn't be any worse for us there than it is here.

AS A SENATOR, SAM HOUSTON CONTINUED TO SPEAK FOR INDIAN RIGHTS IN THE HALLS OF CONGRESS.

What was the result of this extermination policy in Texas? Years of bloody warfare on our exposed frontier!

BUT THE ISSUE OF SLAVERY SOON TESTED THE BONDS OF THE UNION.

The North can't tell us what to do with our slaves.

HOUSTON BECAME UNPOPULAR AS A SENATOR BECAUSE HE WANTED TO PRESERVE THE UNION FIRST AND FOREMOST.

If the Union sinks, let me go down with it.

RETURNING TO TEXAS FROM WASHINGTON, HE STILL HAD ENOUGH SUPPORT TO BE ELECTED GOVERNOR. HE MADE ONLY ONE CAMPAIGN SPEECH.

Preserve Union and you preserve Liberty. They are the same, indivisible.

TROUBLE ERUPTED AT BROWNSVILLE WITH JUAN CORTINA, WHO BELONGED TO AN OLD RANCHING FAMILY.

When I was a kid, this was just another of mama's pastures.

CORTINA MADE A DRAMATIC ENTRANCE INTO THE PUBLIC EYE, SHOOTING THE MARSHAL OF BROWNSVILLE AND SAVING A POOR VAQUERO FROM ARREST.

Gracias mi patron, Gracias!

HE DEFEATED SEVERAL FORCES SENT AGAINST HIM IN WHAT BECAME A POPULAR UPRISING.

AFTER A SIX-MONTH REIGN, CORTINA WAS FORCED TO FLEE INTO THE INTERIOR OF MEXICO BY U.S. TROOPS AND RANGERS UNDER RIP FORD.

Now if he'll just stay there...

TO DISTRACT THE MOVE FOR SECESSION AND UNIFY THE NATION, GOV. HOUSTON PUSHED A GRAND SCHEME.

...a protectorate over Mexico with me at the helm!

HE EVEN TRIED TO TALK ROBERT E. LEE INTO HEADING THE OPERATION, BACKED BY BEN McCULLOCH.

If we had done it after the Mexican War, we wouldn't have had a decade of border headaches.

THE ELECTION OF ABRAHAM LINCOLN AS PRESIDENT DECIDED THE QUESTION OF UNION OR DISUNION FOR THE SOUTH AND DISRUPTED HOUSTON'S PLAN.

This nation cannot exist, half slave and half free.

AT A CONVENTION CALLED IN AUSTIN IN JANUARY 1861 THE ASSEMBLED DELEGATES, LED BY ORAN ROBERTS, DECLARED FOR SECESSION. VOTERS APPROVED THE MEASURE BY FOUR TO ONE.

Under Lincoln our rights in the Union will go unattended.

HOUSTON WOULD NOT TAKE AN OATH TO SUPPORT THE CONFEDERACY AND WAS REMOVED FROM OFFICE.

Sam Houston! Sam Houston!! Come up!

ED CLARK BECAME THE NEW GOVERNOR OF TEXAS JOINED TO THE CONFEDERACY.

TEXANS MARCHED OFF TO BATTLE, THINKING THE WAR WOULD BE A SHORT ONE WITH VICTORY FOR THE SOUTH.

Sam says it's all illegal,

but nobody listens to him anymore.

Whip them ol' Yankees and come home soon, Ned.

BUT IT PROVED OTHERWISE, AND A NUMBER OF PROMINENT TEXANS—MEN SUCH AS BEN McCULLOCH AND ALBERT SIDNEY JOHNSTON—WERE KILLED IN THE FIGHTING.

OTHER MEN STAYED AT HOME TO PROTECT THE FRONTIER.

Somebody has to do it.

EMBOLDENED BY THE LACK OF TROOPS, THE COMANCHES SOUGHT TO REGAIN THEIR LOST TERRITORY.

All the soldiers have gone to fight in the big war—now is our chance!

THEIR RAIDS DEVASTATED THE ENTIRE FRONTIER DURING THE COURSE OF THE CIVIL WAR.

THE SETTLEMENT LINE WAS PUSHED BACK 100 MILES, WITH BURNED OUT HOMES AND HASTILY DUG GRAVES A COMMON SIGHT.

Looks like th' McAlisters stayed too long...

RARELY COULD THE SWIFT RAIDERS BE CAUGHT AND PUNISHED.

Guess we lost 'um again.

WITH TEXAS PORTS BLOCKADED BY THE UNION, MATAMOROS ENJOYED A PROSPEROUS COTTON TRADE.

COTTON TRAFFIC WAS HEAVY IN TOWNS ALL ALONG THE RIO GRANDE, AND THE WEALTH TRICKLED DOWN.

MANY VALLEY TEJANOS JOINED THE CONFEDERACY. SOME, LIKE SANTOS BENAVIDES, FOUGHT IN LOCAL BATTLES.

SPARED THE BRUNT OF MAJOR FIGHTING, TEXAS SETTLED INTO A DULL ROUTINE.

BELTS TIGHTENED AS THE WAR DRAGGED ON.

TEXAN CASUALTIES WERE HIGH BEYOND THE MISSISSIPPI AND WOUNDED VETERANS RETURNED HOME WITH DISCOURAGING NEWS.

ONCE THE SOLDIERS STARTED STRAGGLING BACK, GLOOM AND ANXIETY GRIPPED THE STATE.

ON JUNE 19, 1865, GEN. GRANGER LANDED AT GALVESTON. HE DECLARED FEDERAL AUTHORITY RESTORED AND FREED THE SLAVES, A DAY THAT BECAME CELEBRATED AS JUNETEENTH.

WITHOUT SLAVES, THE LARGE PLANTERS WERE IN TROUBLE.

THE SLAVE OWNERS HOPED THAT INTERIM GOVERNOR A. J. JACK HAMILTON WOULD SET UP A STATE-REGULATED LABOR SYSTEM.

Jack's a Union man, but he's a Texan who understands our problems.

ALL BUT HARD-CORE UNIONISTS WERE DISAPPOINTED.

Slavery is wholly dead and cannot be revised in any form. The North will not allow it.

IN THE NEXT ELECTION JAMES THROCKMORTON BEAT THE RADICAL UNION CANDIDATE ELISHA M. PEASE FOR GOVERNOR.

I attended the secession convention and was one of the few to vote against it.

IN AUGUST 1866 PRESIDENT ANDREW JOHNSON DECLARED THE REBELLION AT AN END IN TEXAS.

We'll soon be one big happy family, just like before.

THROCKMORTON, IN HIS ATTEMPT TO MAINTAIN WHITE CONTROL AND RESTRICT THE FREEDOM OF BLACKS, RAN INTO STIFF OPPOSITION.

These labor codes they've passed amount to slavery in disguise.

ALL THIS POLITICAL BICKERING WAS SWEPT ASIDE WHEN THE U.S. CONGRESS PASSED THE FIRST RECONSTRUCTION ACT IN MARCH 1867. THE NEW REGIMES WERE DECLARED ILLEGAL AND THE SOUTH DIVIDED INTO 5 MILITARY ZONES.

Pres. Johnson used his veto, but it didn't do no good.

PHIL SHERIDAN WAS THE FIRST OF A SERIES OF GENERALS TO HEAD THE FIFTH DISTRICT, WHICH INCLUDED TEXAS.

Texas? Not a fit place to live in from what I hear.

IN JULY THROCKMORTON WAS DECLARED AN IMPEDIMENT TO RECONSTRUCTION AND REPLACED BY THE RADICAL PEASE.

Now we're gonna' see some changes made.

UNDER THE NEW SETUP, THE MILITARY HAD THE POWER TO REMOVE ANY DULY ELECTED PUBLIC OFFICIAL.

We're wiped out Horace. Not a thing we can do.

THE POSTWAR MILITARY GOVERNMENT WAS MUCH RESENTED BY THE BEATEN BUT UNBOWED TEXANS.

The quicker these Rebs learn who won th' war, the quicker we can go home.

KILLINGS SOMETIMES RESULTED, AND A NUMBER OF YOUNG TEXANS HAD TO GO IN HIDING.

THE BLACKS NOW HAD THE RIGHT TO VOTE AND MADE A VALIANT EFFORT TO TAKE CHARGE OF THEIR LIVES.

Education is the way to a better future.

IN 1869 FOURTEEN BLACKS WERE ELECTED TO SERVE IN THE TEXAS LEGISLATURE.

The Freedman's Bureau is improving our situation.

THE EX-SLAVES SOMETIMES SETTLED COMMUNITIES OF THEIR OWN.

Let's call it Peyton Colony, after Mr. Peyton Roberts.

GEN. REYNOLDS ISSUED ORDERS TO CURB VIOLENCE DIRECTED AGAINST BLACKS, UNION MEN, AND U.S. SOLDIERS.

We'll make an example of all murderers.

PRESIDENT GRANT BECAME UPSET WITH THE RESISTANCE FEDERAL FORCES FACED IN TEXAS.

HE SUPPORTED THE TICKET OF E. J. DAVIS IN 1869 AND MADE SURE THAT SOLDIERS GUARDED THE POLLING PLACES.

Things are moving too slow down there to suit me.

DAVIS WON AS GOVERNOR BY A NARROW MARGIN, AND ONE OF HIS FIRST ACTS WAS TO PUSH A POLICE AND MILITIA BILL THROUGH THE LEGISLATURE.

Due to the lawlessness in many parts of Texas, we must take appropriate and timely measures.

TO DO SO, HE HAD TO ARREST AND HOLD CAPTIVE EIGHT OPPOSING SENATORS.

Texas will rue the day this infernal machine was created.

RECRUITS TO THIS STATE POLICE WERE NOT ALWAYS OF THE HIGHEST TYPE.

They'll say it was another attempted escape.

OTHERS, LIKE FUTURE RANGER CAPTAIN LEANDER MCNELLY, DID A GOOD JOB.

I'll crack down on all these feuds.

BUT THE LEGISLATURE DID AWAY WITH THE STATE POLICE IN APRIL 1873, AND FEUDISTS GRADUALLY MADE PEACE.

Maybe we can get some sleep for a change.

41

ENCOURAGED BY THE DEFEAT OF THE POLICE BILL, DEMOCRATS RALLIED TO BEAT GOV. DAVIS AT THE POLLS IN 1873. RICHARD COKE WAS ELECTED.

WHEN DAVIS TRIED TO HAVE THE RESULTS OVERTURNED, THE CAPITAL DIVIDED INTO TWO ARMED CAMPS.

EMBITTERED BY THE FAILURE OF HIS NORTHERN FRIENDS TO SUPPORT HIM, DAVIS YIELDED TO COKE.

RADICAL RECONSTRUCTION WAS OVER. GOV. COKE RE-ESTABLISHED THE TEXAS RANGERS TO RID THE STATE OF HOSTILE INDIANS, RUSTLERS, AND OUTLAWS.

TO SURVIVE THESE HARD TIMES, TEXANS USED THEIR GREATEST NATURAL RESOURCE: WILD CATTLE.

SHORTLY AFTER THE WAR, JOSEPH MCCOY HAD OPENED A MARKET FOR TEXAS CATTLE AT ABILENE, KANSAS.

TEXANS QUICKLY TOOK ADVANTAGE OF MCCOY'S COWTOWN, DRIVING COUNTLESS HERDS UP THE TRAIL AND LATER STOCKING NORTHERN RANCHES.

THE U.S. ARMY COMMENCED VIGOROUS CAMPAIGNS AGAINST THE PLAINS INDIANS. COL. RANALD MACKENZIE WAS AN ABLE COMMANDER.

AFTER MACKENZIE'S SMASHING VICTORY OVER THE COMANCHES AT PALO DURO CANYON IN 1874, CHIEF QUANAH PARKER LED HIS PEOPLE TO RESERVATION LIFE. THEY WERE THE LAST HOLDOUTS.

WITH THE COMING OF THE RAILROAD AND TELEGRAPH, TEXAS ENTERED THE MODERN AGE. THE DISCOVERY OF OIL AND NATURAL GAS CAUSED MORE PROSPERITY, BUT SOME TOWNS PAID A PRICE.

It's either pick up and move or become a ghost town.

ANOTHER ASSET—PUBLIC LAND—PROVIDED THE MONEY FOR A BEAUTIFUL NEW STATE CAPITOL BUILDING, THE SAME WE USE TODAY.

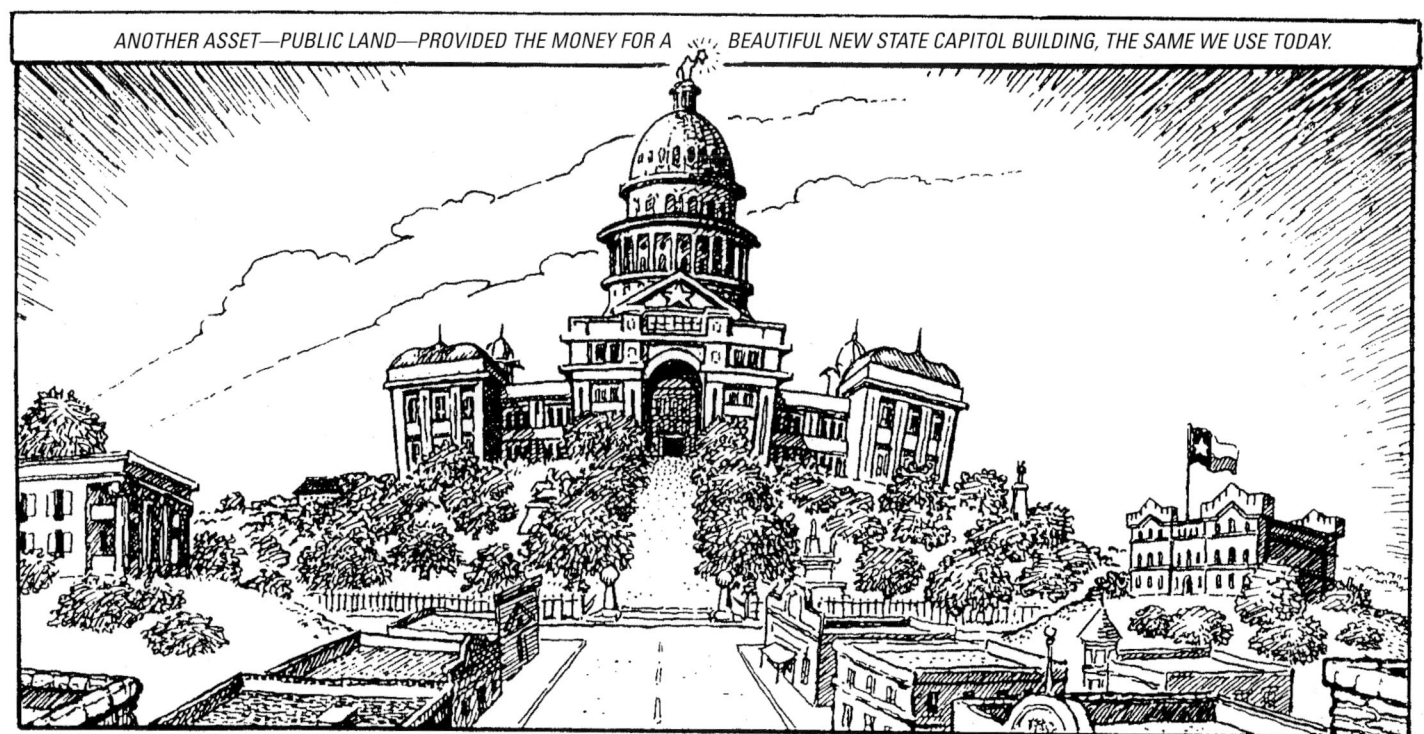

A BIT OF HISTORY ABOUT
Texas History Movies

In the October 3, 1926, edition of the *Dallas Morning News* there appeared a quarter-page advertisement for a "New Educational Art Feature" with the intriguing title *Texas History Movies*. The ad featured a cartoon of Philip Nolan, a mustanger, one of the first Anglo-Americans to penetrate Spanish Texas, under the banner "Wild Horses Dragged 'Em In." Thus was initiated one of the most influential and long-lasting educational comic strip experiments in Texas, if not the entire United States.

Texas History Movies was the concept of E. B. Doran, then director of news and telegraph for the *Dallas News* and the *Dallas Journal*. The title came from J. F. Kimball, a former superintendent of the public schools in Dallas. Jack Patton, a native of Shreveport, Louisiana, born in 1900, was the artist of the strip. Previously he had tried a gag-filled series called "The Restless Years" for the *Journal* and his work continued to grace the pages of the *Morning News* until his retirement in 1961. Handling the text was a Dallas native, John Rosenfield Jr., a University of Texas graduate who was amusements editor for the paper in 1926. Both Patton and Rosenfield were history buffs and shared an obvious delight in the assignment.

Accompanying the "prologue" sequence of the strip in the October 5 edition was an article that set forth what the newspaper hoped to accomplish with its unusual approach: "The News offers this series to its readers with trust that it will be entertaining as

School booklet, 1928. *Courtesy Center for American History, University of Texas at Austin. DI 03039.*

well as educational. Effort has been to make the figures of Texas history living, vital, human figures and not stilted personages. In order that the humanness of the story can be presented, the pictures and text material are at all times colloquial and idiomatic. Such liberties are self confessed."

The article went on to emphasize that these "liberties" did not distort actual facts, which had been carefully researched, but merely accentuated and colored the historical record. Further, the sparse text that accompanied the strip (captions, similar to those in silent movies) had the sole purpose of clarifying or explaining the panels, for it was the creators' aim to "let the pictures tell the story."

Such an approach was revolutionary for 1926, and especially so for boondocks Texas. It expressed an awareness that the lowly comic strip had come of age as an artform in America, distinct from the conventional method of presenting a mass of text, illustrated by several drawings. Here the drawings carried the weight, not the text. The format of the strip was uniform and simple, each daily installment consisting of four panels generally run at the bottom of the paper's second section. It measured a whopping 14 inches across and was set apart from other syndicated strips. Reflecting the old work-for-hire mentality, credit to neither artist nor writer was given and copyright was vested in the publisher of the *News*, A. H. Belo Corporation. The creators, however, would soon get their due because of the strip's popularity.

As an added incentive for its younger readers, the paper offered a prize of five dollars for the best answers to ten questions posed about each weekly installment of the strip. Five dollars was a lot of money in 1926, especially for kids in elementary school. The hope was expressed that, if school children followed the series, they would "acquire a priceless knowledge of their state and a love for its traditions." Follow it they did, and with a devotion little imagined when the strip was launched. *Texas History Movies* ran continuously in the *Dallas Morning News* until June of 1927, when—by request of history teachers all over the state—it was suspended until the following fall, when school resumed. By the time the series ended on June 9, 1928, its creators had logged over 1,600 panels (428 daily installments) and greatly influenced the way that Texans would perceive their historical heritage. Adults loved the series as much as the kids, and its appeal to "Young and Old" guaranteed that the cartoon strip would not be forgotten any time soon.

No sooner did the series end than efforts to perpetuate its influence began. In 1928 the P. L. Turner Company of Dallas, a noted textbook publisher, bought hardcover rights to the strip. Under imprint of The Southwest Press, Turner that year released the first compilation of *Movies* in its entirety, running 217 pages. Deservedly so, Patton received credit for the illustrations and Rosenfield for the text. The book's foreword by them reaffirmed their purpose of keeping the stories "humorous, human,

Sample page, at actual size, from the 1928 school booklet. *Courtesy Center for American History, University of Texas at Austin. DI 03040.*

vivid, and real." It also defended their use of "slang, colloquialisms, modernisms, and deliberate anachronisms" to capture what they believed to be "the spirit of an episode." This 1928 first edition (done in blue ink) is now extremely rare, though it gave birth to many subsequent printings.

That same year the Magnolia Petroleum Company, "prompted by a desire to be of service to

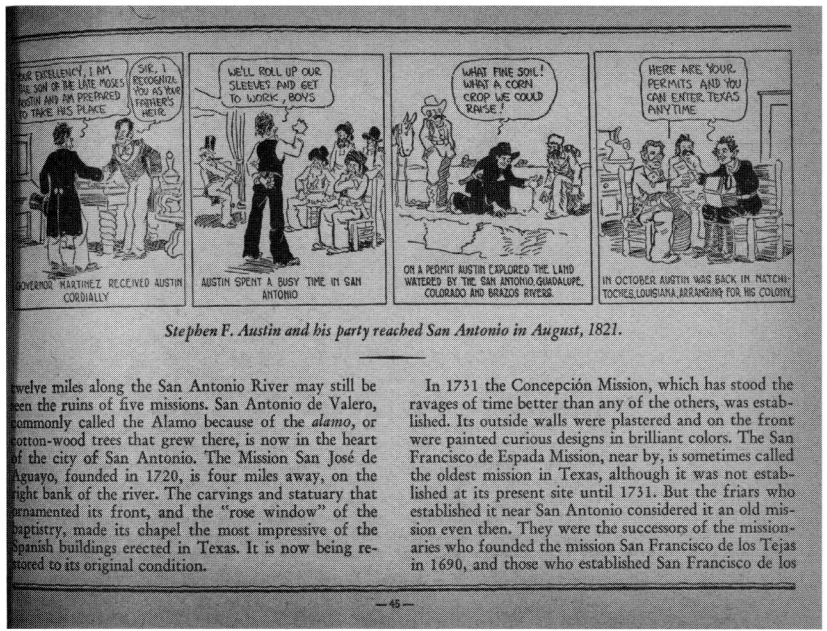

Page from 1935 edition, showing disjunction between text and art. *Courtesy Center for American History, University of Texas at Austin. DI 03042.*

the pupils of the public schools of Texas and to have some small part in helping impress upon them the remarkable past of their state," made an arrangement with the Turner Company to print an abridged version. It ran 64 pages and ended with the battle of San Jacinto. The booklet was later expanded to 128 pages and some version of it was given to the schools free of charge for three decades until millions of copies had been distributed. The amazing thing is that this booklet was in circulation in Texas some years before comic books, as we now know them, had been "invented" in America!

The hardcover edition was large, measuring 9 by 12 inches. It had a bold cover design with title at the top, curtains drawn back, and a scene from the battle of the Alamo on the screen. At the bottom sat an enthralled audience. This design was also on the cover of the school booklet, only 5 by 7 inches. In other words, the reader was at the "movies" and each panel represented a frozen scene or frame from the larger story's movie reel. Patton and Rosenfield made reference to this technique in their foreword: "Thus the pictures themselves tell the story and not the printed captions, which serve in the fashion of cinema sub-titles." As a tribute to their creation, we have kept the same title on this complete revision of the story in graphic form.

Both the hardcover and the booklet—despite their size difference—had the same page arrangement. Two newspaper installments (eight panels) graced each page. They made a three-panel frame on the page with Rosenfield's brief explanation in the middle. We have reproduced a sample page from the 1928 booklet at actual size—so small it is a miracle that Texas school children didn't damage their eyesight reading the thing. Patton's art work might have helped because his pictures were clean and simple, yet packed with suggestive detail and expressive movement. Jack Patton had a knack for giving the eye all the essentials needed to comprehend the event portrayed without cluttering his panels. Studying his work, it is not surprising that *Movies* captured the imagination of Texans for generations.

In 1943 Magnolia purchased the copyright to the booklet, with the Turner Company retaining publication rights to the larger book. The booklet cover design changed several times, but most were red and blue with a Texas flag and several panels of Patton's art. One notable change came in 1935 with a different format, lengthwise 9 inches, 6 inches tall, and the addition of some text by "one of the foremost historians of the state." In this edition there were four panels at the top with the text below and taking up as much space as the art. One big problem was that the new text described events far behind the art on the same page. As an example the text talks about the founding of missions at San Antonio in 1731 while Patton's art shows Stephen F. Austin's arrival in Texas in 1821. This was poor planning that made the story harder to follow. In this edition a Part Two has been added on the "Industrial Development of Texas" extending the overall length to 128 pages. By the 1950s the booklet was issued under Magnolia Petroleum's more familiar Mobil logo featuring the "Flying Red Horse." It was back to the 5 by 7 inch digest format but twice the size of the original school edition, containing 248 newspaper strips in 128 pages instead of 124 strips in 64 pages.

In 1959, the year I graduated from Stockdale High School in South Texas, Magnolia merged with Socony-Mobil, a global operation that extended far beyond the borders of Texas. Consequently, a decision was made to discontinue publication of the little comic book that had shaped the minds of several generations of Texas school children. The exact reasons for this decision vary. Some say that "economy measures" were a factor. Others point out that after Magnolia became Mobil and went national it could no longer justify providing a free booklet for Texas school children without doing the same for kids in all the other states.

Another reason for Mobil's decision cannot be ignored, however, and that is the comic book's depiction of ethnic minorities and the increasing criticism that the oil company was receiving because of it. Clearly what had passed for legitimate humor in the 1920s was becoming more offensive to growing numbers of Texans. Particularly offended were Hispanics, especially ex-servicemen who had served their country during World War II and the Korean conflict. Upon returning home they protested the way in which *Texas History Movies* treated Mexicans, criticisms that many Anglos had to admit were valid. In addition to the generally unfavorable way that Mexicans were visually depicted by Patton, Rosenfield's captions and talk balloons sometimes contained racial slurs. Indians said "Ugh" and not much else, except to remark how tough and what good shots the "Pale-Faces" were. Blacks fared even worse, typical of the accepted cartoon stereotypes of the 1920s. In fairness to Patton, it should be noted that many of his Anglos were drawn as scruffy, unsavory characters of bad behavior.

Whatever the actual reason, in 1960 Mobil Oil ceased distribution and donated its copyright to the Texas State Historical Association (TSHA). Believing the booklet still had some merit and certainly a historical significance, Fred H. Moore, president of Mobil North America and a friend of the Association, made the actual bequest.

Meanwhile, the P. L. Turner Company had continued, since 1928, to issue a number of hardcover editions. The cover was usually green, sometimes with the movie theatre illustration laminated in a frame, sometimes without. One issue came in 1935, known as the "Centennial Edition," celebrating Texas's 100th birthday the next year. It ran 244 pages instead of the usual 217. Turner's last edition came in 1963, packaged with a selection of reading material by Bertha Mae Cox and titled *Let's Read About Texas*. This print run lasted until 1968. As with the school booklets, it is difficult to assign a year to these hardcover editions because they often list a string of copyright dates going back to the beginning. I have only seen three different examples of the school booklet's contents, even though the covers changed with various printings.

A company called Graphic Ideas, under the leadership of Jim Box, acquired the Turner Company's rights and brought out a 1970 hardcover edition with "fresh" text by Orlo Mitchell of Houston. Mitchell, while admitting that Patton-Rosenfield had skipped important sequences of Texas history (like the wanderings of Cabeza de Vaca), left the original sequence intact. Nor were the racial slurs that had so annoyed Hispanics taken out. The format remained the same—eight panels to a page—with Mitchell's new text placed in the center. At least it described the art on the same page. This was the last edition before *Texas History Movies* underwent drastic revision by both copyright holders to bring it in line with modern ethnic perceptions.

The TSHA, upon receiving copyright to the booklet version in 1961, knew that Mobil had caught some flak from Hispanics over the "image" that the book projected. It was sensitive to the changes that would be necessary if the state's oldest learned society was to play any part in the continued use of *Movies* in the public schools. In 1969 a group called the Texas History Education Advisory Committee was organized to "revitalize" the teaching of Texas history. High priority was given by this elite group of educators to the old *Movies* booklet, for its value as a teaching aid had long been recognized.

An article by Jack Loftis in the Sunday supplement of the *Houston Chronicle*, February 28, 1971, noted that the TSHA was planning to reissue the classic with "minor changes" to those panels that various ethnic groups might find offensive. This version appeared in 1974, called *Texas History Illustrated*, and the changes were far more than minor. Although an "Editorial Advisory Board" of three Hispanic males and a black woman was selected for input, it appears that most of the objectionable points were mulled over and decided by Dr. L. Tuffly Ellis, head of the TSHA at the time, and his assistant, Dr. Kenneth Ragsdale. Changes—both in art and dialogue—were then forwarded to the *Houston Chronicle*, which had offered to do the printing and provide technical help. To avoid identification with the old, biased version, Dr. Ellis suggested the new title *Illustrated*.

This 1974 TSHA edition is printed on common newsprint, measuring 7 by 10 inches and 55 pages in length. There are two rows of four panels on each page, and the text remained the same as in Mobil's 1935 booklet except for a few corrections of historical accuracy. This, again, meant that the text had nothing to do with the art, a shortcoming that should have been recognized and fixed. The booklet had an initial printing of 50,000 copies, followed by another 50,000 with a grant from the Texas Educational Association. In 1986 yet another printing was done, with better paper and a glossy two-color cover. Although the title was changed back to *Texas History Movies*, the content is the same as the revised edition of 1974. In his introduction George B. Ward of the TSHA proudly noted that of 100,000 copies distributed to Texas schools, not one complaint had been received.

The TSHA was not alone in its revision process. The hardcover rights that had passed from the Turner Company to Graphic Ideas were acquired in 1981 by Pepper Jones Martinez, Inc., of Dallas (PJM). They issued a $250 facsimile of the Turner original—in blue ink—in 1984. It now sells for a fraction of the cost and is the edition often seen in used book stores. For one who wishes to examine the unexpurgated original, and discover what all the fuss is about, this is the most accessible route. In 1986 PJM brought out a soft cover "Sesquicentennial Edition" booklet reasonably priced at $5.95. It contained 155 pages in the lengthwise format, also in blue ink, and Dr. Joe B. Frantz, a noted historian and former TSHA director, was hired to write a new text. PJM optimistically printed 150,000 copies of the booklet but it failed to receive the Sesquicentennial Committee's official seal of approval. Sales suffered as a result, especially orders that might have gone to various school districts. PJM did not help its case by adding some controversial panels on Santa Anna's mock marriage at San Antonio and how he was caught at San Jacinto literally with his pants down, which caused him to lose the battle—and Texas.

When I first read *Texas History Movies* in school I was a budding artist and the booklet was a great inspiration to me. It told me about events that had happened long ago and stimulated an interest in our historical heritage as Texans. Coming home after school I wandered the countryside and imagined ferocious Indians behind every bush. Other times I was an Indian myself, complete with my homemade bow and arrows. Real arrowheads picked up on my roamings were proof that these people had once lived here. Where had they gone? Even with its cartoony treatment *Texas History Movies* suggested the answer: They had been killed or driven out in years of violent struggle. A few managed to survive and blend in with the larger society, but it took me awhile to learn this and meet their descendants.

In time I decided to draw my own version of these events in a more realistic style than Jack Patton. My object was to create a "time machine" effect that would make the readers feel like they were there when the events occurred. This requires a lot of research, which I did anyway to get the story right. But I borrowed freely from Patton-Rosenfield, especially their use of slang to make my characters real human beings instead of lofty cardboard figures that few of us can identify with. When possible I tried to inject humor, for it is a painless way to learn about the past and appreciate the long distance we have traveled to reach our present prospects for the 21st century.

I hope that my rendition of the old classic, *Texas History Movies*, will "grab" a few young minds and make them want to learn more about the interesting people and events briefly touched on in this booklet.

Jack Jackson,
Austin, Texas